OTHER BOOKS BY
LEONA ROSTENBERG AND MADELEINE STERN

BY LEONA ROSTENBERG

English Publishers in the Graphic Arts 1599–1700
Literary, Political, Scientific, Religious & Legal Publishing,
  Printing & Bookselling in England, 1551–1700 (2 volumes)
The Minority Press & The English Crown: A Study in
  Repression 1558–1625
The Library of Robert Hooke: The Scientific Book Trade
  of Restoration England
Bibliately: The History of Books on Postage Stamps

BY LEONA ROSTENBERG AND MADELEINE B. STERN

Bookman's Quintet: Five Catalogues about Books
Old & Rare: Forty Years in the Book Business
Between Boards: New Thoughts on Old Books
Quest Book—Guest Book: A Biblio-Folly
Connections: Our Selves—Our Books
Old Books in the Old World: Reminiscences of Book Buying
  Abroad
Old Books, Rare Friends: Two Literary Sleuths and
  Their Shared Passion
New Worlds in Old Books
Books Have Their Fates

BY MADELEINE STERN

We Are Taken
The Life of Margaret Fuller
Louisa May Alcott
Purple Passage: The Life of Mrs. Frank Leslie
Imprints on History: Book Publishers and American Frontiers
We the Women: Career Firsts of Nineteenth-Century America
So Much in a Lifetime: The Life of Dr. Isabel Barrows

Queen of Publishers' Row: Mrs. Frank Leslie
The Pantarch: A Biography of Stephen Pearl Andrews
Heads & Headlines: The Phrenological Fowlers
Books and Book People in Nineteenth-Century America
Antiquarian Bookselling in the United States: A History
Louisa May Alcott: From Blood & Thunder to Hearth & Home

EDITED BY MADELEINE B. STERN

Women on the Move (4 volumes)
The Victoria Woodhull Reader
Behind a Mask: The Unknown Thrillers of Louisa May Alcott
*Plots and Counterplots: More Unknown Thrillers of Louisa
    May Alcott*
*Publishers for Mass Entertainment in Nineteenth-Century
    America*
A Phrenological Dictionary of Nineteenth-Century Americans
Critical Essays on Louisa May Alcott
*A Modern Mephistopheles and Taming a Tartar by
    Louisa M. Alcott*
Louisa May Alcott Unmasked: Collected Thrillers
Modern Magic
The Feminist Alcott: Stories of a Woman's Power

CO-EDITED BY MADELEINE B. STERN

*Selected Letters of Louisa May Alcott (with Joel Myerson
    and Daniel Shealy)*
*A Double Life: Newly Discovered Thrillers of Louisa May
    Alcott (with Myerson and Shealy)*
The Journals of Louisa May Alcott (with Myerson and Shealy)
Louisa May Alcott: Selected Fiction (with Myerson and Shealy)
*Freaks of Genius: Unknown Thrillers of Louisa May Alcott
    (with Shealy and Myerson)*
*From Jo March's Attic: Stories of Intrigue and Suspense
    (with Shealy)*

Leona Rostenberg
Madeleine Stern

BOOK ENDS

Two Women,
One Enduring Friendship

THE FREE PRESS
New York   London   Toronto   Sydney   Singapore

ƒP

THE FREE PRESS
A Division of Simon & Schuster, Inc.
1230 Avenue of the Americas
New York, NY 10020

Designed by Deirdre C. Amthor

Manufactured in the United States of America

10   9   8   7   6   5   4   3   2   1

Library of Congress Cataloging-in-Publication Data
Rostenberg, Leona.
   Bookends: two women, one enduring friendship.
   Leona Rostenberg and Madeleine Stern.
       p. cm.
   Includes index.
   1. Rostenberg, Leona. 2. Stern, Madeleine B., 1912–.
   3. Antiquarian booksellers—United States—Biography.
   4. Book collectors—United States—Biography. I. Stern,
   Madeleine B., 1912–. II. Title.

Z473.R77 R64 2001
381'.45002'092273—dc-21
[B]   2001023061

ISBN 0-7432-0245-7

To Helen Keppler Miller

Our Friend for All Seasons in Years Past and Present

CONTENTS

PRELUDE

We were always pioneers, we were told—at first alone and then together. In one way or another we explored what had not been explored—as children walking unfamiliar streets, as women researching the unstudied, thinking independently, living differently.

We were pioneers in a century that survived many radical transformations. In its beginning it was shadowed, embraced by the affirmations and certainties of the nineteenth century. Our century lost its certitude and yielded to the naysayers early and suddenly when a tragedy at sea taught it that nothing is invincible, nothing is indestructible, nothing is "unsinkable." Two wars and a Holocaust shaped the first half of our century, and in the seesaw of doubt and hope that followed, it was doubt that often prevailed. Against such a background we two walked together and fashioned our lives a bit ahead of established custom and accepted convention—walked, they said, as pioneers.

That century has ended now, and with it our place in the vanguard. We are no longer explorers, no longer pioneers. The world we once explored is on its way to oblivion, its landmarks lost in mist.

The landscape is no longer familiar. Its streets have lost their identity for us. Its clothing is not ours. Even its language is foreign, pervaded by phrases we cannot translate—dot com or dot org. . . . We who were once pioneers have been thrown off course; "new-ness" manipulated by interlopers is metamorphosing our lives. But perhaps if we meet these challenges head-on, face-to-face, the intruders will lose their hold and we will regain our way, forging it as we go, out of the old century and into the new. And, in the process, reclaim for ourselves our role as pioneers.

Some day soon, we shall try to find our way through the computer world. We shall walk the web to a paradise of information retrieval. We shall enroll in an Internet student program and develop an Internet Web site presence. We shall learn a new language and participate in a new ideology. Moreover, into that realm, still strange to us, we shall carry the Age of the Book, which we know so well. We shall pioneer by linking the two great discoveries, the two great eras of our millennium. Some day soon.

This we can and will do. What we cannot do is accept another and quite different event that afflicts us all, but that looms especially with increasing years. We cannot accept, we can scarcely face, we can barely contemplate the ending of life. We who are advancing toward that end must first experience the end of those we loved. There is no compromise here, and often no satisfactory explanation of why we cannot live forever. All we can do toward acceptance of the ineluctible is remember, recall those we have loved, restore their beginnings, reanimate the past, and so live it again. This we propose to do.

Adolescentia, Jacobus Wimpheling, Latin, 1508

One of the earliest works on the training of youth by a noted Strasbourg humanist, who advises adolescents about their studies, their readings, their ethical and religious conduct.

Headstart in 1508. With three full-page woodcuts, bound in oxblood morocco, with the arms of Stirling-Maxwell, distinguished English collector.

Acquired by a colleague, 1967

Chapter One
BEGINNINGS

The two pictures are the same size, their dimensions identical. Although the photos were taken separately, in studios far removed from each other, and at different times—one in 1910, the other in 1915—they would have fitted together perfectly. One day, at the end of the century, they would be so framed, side by side.

The earlier portrait was of Leona, age two, the other of Madeleine, age three. The photographers, whoever they were, had posed their subjects alike. Both children faced the camera, looking to the left. Both were seated in similar round-backed chairs. And both registered their differing reactions to what they seemed to be reading—Leona, the newsprint of 1910; Madeleine, that of 1915. As the century was closing, to illustrate a book they had co-authored, they brought together the two pictures. They, like their subjects, had grown together apart.

The growing together as well as the apartness had begun long before the portraits were taken. The reaching toward each other, along with the parallels in their lives, began before we were born. And when we were born, so we were told, the rejoicing of our parents, especially our mothers, echoed each other.

The similarities didn't end there; each mother already had a son. Leona was born with a three-year-old brother, Madeleine with a nine-year-old brother. Each mother yearned for a daughter. Each had difficulty in giving birth. Leona's mother, Louisa, had suffered several miscarriages; Madeleine's mother, Lillie, had been warned at Leonard's birth not to have another child. Besides, each woman was beyond the normal age of child-bearing. Both of them must have feared another pregnancy and intoned hallelujahs after the event. The mothers, it seems, shared more than the first letter of their given names.

That kind of sharing, of paralleling, runs like bright thread through the fabric of our two families from their earliest beginnings.

LEONA

We can both trace our family origins back to late eighteenth-century Germany. I am especially fortunate, since I still have the Letter Book of my maternal great-grandfather, and through it he comes alive for me. He did not immigrate to America, but he was the font of the family emigration. He must have been a remarkable man—a man of independent convictions, forthright, without pretense. David Dreyfus of Ingenheim, Germany, a miller by trade, was born with the nineteenth century. His crop of curly bright red hair earned him the sobriquet "Der roter David." As he ground wheat from grain, so he shaped his children into stalwart human beings.

After marrying Leah Johanna Frank in 1835, he sired a large brood, to whom he tried to impart his individualism. He himself practiced his own form of Thoreauvian disobedience. He upheld those tenets of Judaism that he chose to uphold, observing the Sabbath and the Holy Days, but when ordered by the authorities to send his sons to Jewish Sabbath School for religious instruction, he refused. Offered the choice of paying a fine or being confined in the local jail, he chose the latter. David Dreyfus was his own man.

His eldest son, Theodore, inherited his father's principles—"Remain true to your faith and never pretend piety"—and received a fatherly blessing when, at the age of sixteen, he departed for New York, the first of the family to settle in America. My grandfather, Leon Dreyfus, was the next son to make the overseas adventure.

The lure of that adventure was spreading like a contagion among young Europeans during the 1840s and 1850s, partially as a result of the Revolution of 1848, partially as a reaction to growing German militarism and the insidious spread of anti-Semitism. A life in Ingenheim devoted to converting grain into wheat, with a required period of army service, offered little future, especially when it was punctuated with subtle disdain or outright mistreatment for Jews. In hamlets of the Palatinate, tales of American streets free to all and paved with gold became irresistible temptations to youngsters of Heuchelheim or Billingheim or Ingenheim. Leon Dreyfus, born in

1842 and coming to maturity during that period, joined the rising wave of emigration and, at the age of seventeen, set forth, not for New York but for New Orleans.

New Orleans was a far cry from Ingenheim, but young Leon Dreyfus did not feel an alien for long. His sister Maria had arrived there before him and married Nathan Koch, a jeweler. As a result, Leon was not intimidated by the city's unfamiliar aspects, its large black population, its exotic French Quarter. The brown-eyed, dark-haired young man found a home immediately with the family and soon enrolled for a course at George Soule's Commercial College. The certificate he was awarded is of interest less for its text than for its date: 18 January 1860. The country was on the brink of the War between the States. Leon Dreyfus, preparing to join his brother-in-law's jewelry firm, was not prepared to endorse the Confederate cause. The concept of slavery was as abhorrent to him as the reality. Secession he deplored. Nonetheless, as he matured, he kept his opinions to himself and to his family, worked hard, and by the time the war was over had become a partner in the restyled

N. Koch and L. Dreyfus, Wholesale Dealers in Watches, Jewelry, Clocks, Spectacles, Jewelry Boxes, Watchmakers, and Jewelry Tools and Materials. Although there was no mention in its comprehensive title, the firm at 18 Chartres Street also dealt in tiaras, one of which, said to have been worn at Napoleon's second marriage, was purchased from a French traveler and eventually came into my possession.

Shortly before he gained his partnership, Leon became a "Citizen of the United States." His naturalization papers, dated 1 May 1866, are in my desk. My future grandfather gave me far more than his name. Soon the life of this young German-American would change. Two years after attaining his citizenship, he traveled abroad to see his parents at Heuchelheim and to acquire merchandise in London for his firm. There he met his future wife, Bertha Hirsch, my grandmother.

Bertha of course was related to Leon. German-born Jews, notoriously inbred, fervently believed in keeping the family intact and unadulterated. They seldom hesitated to marry nieces or cousins, confident that their lineage would be improved by the process.

Certainly Bertha's life was remarkable. Born in Mainz, she was raised as a Jew but was sent to a local convent school as a day student. She was fluent in French and also an avid devourer of the German classics, and even after she became a grandmother, she spouted lines from Goethe and Schiller, Lessing and Heine. Meanwhile, her family had moved to London where, at the age of twenty-four, she met the twenty-six-year-old suitor from distant New Orleans.

In 1868, Bertha set sail for the city on the Mississippi, and the next year she and Leon were married in the Reform Jewish temple, Shangarai Chassed. Surely they were aware of the overwhelming problems of Reconstruction, although, as members of the growing German colony of New Orleans, for the most part they kept to themselves. They might take an occasional carriage drive to West End or Spanish Fort, or enjoy fireworks or a musicale, but by and large they led a German life in the Franco-American city, attending the German opera house, reading the German newspapers.

The Americanization of my grandparents was a gradual process. When the Reform Temple Sinai was founded under the ministry of a rabbi from New York's Temple Emanu-El, which one day Madeleine's family would attend, Leon and Bertha joined it. Eventually, they affiliated themselves with the less sectarian philosophy of Felix Adler, founder of Ethical Culture. The English language took the place of German in their conversation. In their homes on Thalia Street and, later, Magazine Street, their American children were born.

The first was Louisa, born in 1870. Louisa was a product of German and American culture, a Southern belle but also a woman of the world. Louisa became my adored and irreplaceable mother.

MADELEINE

Four lifesize portraits hang today on our walls. More than anything I have read or heard, they carry me back to the past. Two are signed by the painter, a German named Thieme; the other two, unsigned, were in all probability the work of an itinerant artist. Armed with brush and palette, the artist wandered from town to town, from hamlet to hamlet, offering to

pose and paint merchant or miller, banker or trades-
man and spouse. In Germany he wandered from the
Palatinate, where he doubtless passed through Ingenheim, offering his services to Leona's forebears, south
to Bavaria, where he offered them to mine. My great-
grandparents, living in the small town of Altenkun-
stadt, near Munich, accepted and posed for their
portraits in the early 1850s.

The great-grandparent with the intimidating
name of Wolf Mack had an arresting face crowned
with white hair. He died in 1854, at which time his
courageous wife, Justine, left Germany with her children and sailed to America. Justine's portrait shows a
remarkable woman in exotic attire, elaborately
adorned with jewels and ornaments. She would live
several years in an alien country and die in the city of
Cincinnati, Ohio.

The other two great-grandparents settled eventually in New York City, and there is even a possibility
that their unsigned portraits were painted not in Germany but in the States. Husband and wife were related, of course, following the custom of Jewish
families, most of whom espoused intermarriage. They

are not as elaborately clothed as the other pair. They look out forthrightly from the canvases and seem quite comfortable in their large armchairs. My great-grandfather Isaac Rauh, attired in black, wears a signet ring; my great-grandmother Magdalena, a bracelet and brooch, all of which are now mine. This great-grandmother had been a Mack before her marriage. Their daughter Rosa Rauh would, when her turn came, marry a Mack. The intertwining, the connections, persisted.

I would be named after my great-grandmother Magdalena. She lived until my mother was ten years old, and my mother loved her dearly; she often told me that she would spend the night at her grandmother's home and be given extra-special sandwiches to take to school. "Oh, I see you spent the night at your grandma's," commented a schoolmate, eyeing the tasty concoction.

The name Mack had been adopted by my forebears when Napoleon ruled Europe and ordained that Jews take surnames for themselves. The name was fashioned from the initials of one ancestor's former appellation: *Moishe Aus Kups.* The Jew Moishe lived in Kups and, at the beginning of the nineteenth century, became Mack—a name that would continue in the New World.

My grandfather Leonard Mack was married to Rosa Rau—she had apparently dropped the silent *h* from her surname—on April 18, 1864, before the end of the Civil War. They were married by a minister of the Temple Emanu-El of the City of New York—not the same rabbi who had married Leona's grandparents, but certainly one who was well acquainted with him.

Early in their married life, probably after the birth of their two oldest children, my grandparents moved from New York to Cincinnati, where an already large Jewish colony, including my great-grandmother Justine, was becoming larger and more influential. The city on the shore of the Ohio River offered the Jewish émigrés in the mid-nineteenth century not only opportunity for advancement, but the attraction of the familiar. Kin gathered together, a bulwark against a sometimes unfriendly world. It is said that by the time of the Civil War, when Leona's grandfather was evincing antislavery sentiments, a few Macks were involved in a cotton-buying deal with General Grant's father, Jesse. The incident, which ended in a lawsuit that was thrown out of court, and which may have prompted General Grant to issue his anti-Semitic General Orders No. 11 in December 1862, is the subject of an article entitled "Anti-Semitism in Lincoln's Time."

Despite the Civil War and the restrictions it imposed, Leonard Mack's liquor business continued, and after the war was over it prospered beyond his expectations. In 1870 Rosa was again pregnant, and in anticipation of the new birth, Leonard presented his wife with a specially beautiful piece of jewelry. At one of the socials organized by the Cincinnati Reform temple, he had met a traveling salesman who represented the New Orleans firm of Koch and Dreyfus. It was from that firm that the jewel—a ruby ring set in gold—was purchased for presentation to the expectant mother. Leonard did not, could not, know what links were being forged.

On July 17, 1871, Rosa Rau Mack gave birth to twins, a boy and a girl. Thanks to the growth of her husband's business, she allowed herself to contemplate seriously a change she had apparently long hoped for.

Family tradition preserves her priceless remark: "I'd rather be a lamppost in New York than the mayor of Cincinnati."

When the twins were six months old, the family resettled in that dreamed-of city. One of the twins, Lillie Mack, would become a woman of extraordinary understanding, the mother whose boundless love shaped my life.

LEONA

My grandfather Leon Dreyfus, who was one of eight children, sired eight children. His oldest, Louisa, my mother, was a spoiled darling. A beautiful, extremely feminine little girl, she loved to play-act, a passion she never lost. The first big event in little Lou's life took place in 1873, when the family, including three children, went abroad. In London and Ingenheim the youngsters were shown off to their grandparents. Pictures of Louisa show her standing on a velvet chair, wearing a scalloped skirt, earrings quite prominent, and ringlets encircling her lovely oval face.

The young Louisa comes alive not only through

pictures but through the letters written to her by a dot-
ing father. In 1877, when she was seven, Leon journeyed to New York on business and sent notes to his
favorite. A few years later his "dear Louisechen" received letters sent from New York's Union Square Hotel, inquiring about her "new teachers" and asking,
"Do you practice music and drawing regularly?" By
this time Louisa was attending a private academy with
her sister Josephine, excelling in elocution and story-
telling rather than in mathematics and science. As for
acting, she never ceased her performances, and as she
matured she starred in amateur theatricals and cha-
rades. At New Orleans masques and balls Louisa was
always the center of a circle of admiring and attentive
beaux. Her tendency to flirt manifested itself early and
would persist, along with a reluctance to form a permanent relationship. She was a dabbler in romance.

In 1888, with the growing success of Koch and
Dreyfus, Leon planned to move both firm and family to
New York. Louisa, eighteen years old, was under-
standably reluctant to leave her bevy of young men and
the audiences who applauded her stirring elocution.
She was rapidly developing into a Southern belle and

was unsure of how the northern metropolis would re-act to a young New Orleans woman. Apparently she became reconciled to the move, and her father wrote to her from New York in September 1888: "I am pleased to hear it, and am in hopes all of us will in a short time get to like the mode of life here and the people of New York. It would be to your advantage if you would con-tinue the studies of literature, elocution and drawing."

Before the exodus to New York, Louisa pur-chased *A Galaxy Album* "especially adapted for auto-graphs & sketches," bound in red calf with a gilt floral motif and stamped title. When family and friends gathered for farewells, they penned their mementos, wishing the sparkling Miss Dreyfus Godspeed from "the sunny South" along with "the luxuries of a wise contentment and the happiness of a beautiful life." The autographed testimony to the attractions of a Southern belle went with her to New York.

In July 1889, the family entrained for the north, a journey of three days and two nights. By August they were settled in a brownstone at 45 East 92nd Street, just off Madison Avenue. As for the jewelry business now set up on Maiden Lane, it prospered, and to meet the company's commitments, an enlarged staff of travelers was recruited "to be dispatched to all sections of the country," including Cincinnati, where no doubt several members of the Mack family became customers of Koch and Dreyfus. The success of Koch and Dreyfus, however, could not withstand the effects of the national panic of 1893. Its liabilities mounted as it sustained heavy losses from overexpansion, and by 1897 it ceased to exist. A year later, Leon Dreyfus died of a massive heart attack.

His charming eldest daughter had been spared some of the family anxieties. In 1894, at the invitation of her father's sister, she traveled abroad, visiting the family in Ingenheim and Heuchelheim. From that trip a permanent and radiant memento hangs upon our wall above the fireplace.

Before the family's departure for New York, Louisa had had occasional visits with a first cousin who lived in Hattiesburg, Mississippi. Cousin Rachel had artistic aspirations, and during a visit to Berlin, where she studied art, she met and married a German physician. Not long after, gossip about the young painter leaked across the seas. Cousin Rachel had abandoned her husband to live with a French artist. Flirtatious Louisa was intrigued by the whispered stories of her cousin's free lifestyle, and while she was in Germany, she arranged to visit Cousin Rachel in Berlin.

When Rachel eyed her charming and beautiful cousin, now twenty-four years old, she immediately posed her for a portrait. She draped a fur-trimmed piano cover over Louisa's shoulder and took up her paintbrush. The result shows a vivacious yet serene young woman in profile, hair parted in the middle, deep brown eyes gazing into eternity. Louisa brought the canvas home for framing and, during the months that followed, must often have looked back longingly to the time she sat for her portrait.

She had returned home to continued national panic and insecurity. Ill equipped to add to the family income, she nonetheless needed some kind of work and self-fulfillment. Her parents were members of the Reform Temple Bethel and ardently admired its minister, Rabbi Kaufmann Kohler. The rabbi suggested that Louisa volunteer her services for the Cherry Street school, one of the charities sponsored by the temple. Located on the Lower East Side, the school was a haven for the children of refugees from Russian pogroms—the "huddled masses yearning to breathe free." Louisa, helping them with the English language, helped them also to "breathe free." In addition, she widened her own circle by meeting other volunteer teachers, one of whom, a member of Temple Emanu-El, was named Lillie Mack.

Lillie Mack was no Southern belle. Nonetheless she had much in common with Louisa Dreyfus, although the two women would not become close friends until the latter part of their lives.

MADELEINE

On July 17, 1871, the arrival of twins doubled the family of Rosa and Leonard Mack. An older brother, Will, and an older sister, Anna, had preceded them. Six months after the twins' birth, the Macks moved to New York and occupied a brownstone in the West forties. One set of grandparents—Magdalena and Isaac Rauh—was on hand to offer much-needed help and support, and Leonard Mack's liquor business seemed to be prospering.

At all events, by the time she was six or seven, Lillie was sent to Froelich's school, where modern pedagogical principles were practiced. As the little girl with intense brown eyes and regular features learned her letters, she began to develop a love of books and reading that she would pass on one day to her daughter. In the late 1870s and early 1880s, Manhattan was developing almost as rapidly as Lillie Mack, and while walking to school she could observe its changing skyline. On her way to Froelich's she watched the building of St. Patrick's Cathedral and learned to love the vibrant, ever expanding city.

By the time Lillie Mack was in her early teens, the family moved north to a somewhat remote, countrified area called Harlem. At that time, long before the Harlem Renaissance, the area attracted to its quiet brownstones a host of German-American Jews most comfortable with one another; 133 West 126th Street, between Lenox and Seventh Avenues, was just another brownstone in a street of brownstones. It became a warm and comforting place in which to grow to maturity. Although Lillie was never very close to her twin—she was more his opposite than his duplicate—she tolerated Louis, as he tolerated her. Having an older brother and sister at hand must have been protective, at least early on.

Lillie's mother provided her young daughter with more than protection and more than love. When Rosa had arrived in this country, at the age of twelve, with her parents, she was sent to a school that proved restrictive and at times threatening. Instead of encouraging Rosa, her teacher mocked her German accent in class. At this the child gathered her books together and threw them at the offending instructor. Later she would impart her bold independence to Lillie.

If she loved her mother, that daughter adored her father. A gentle man in every way, he was tender and devoted to his children and almost equally devoted to his garden. The peach tree he planted in his backyard would long survive him, and as for his border of lilies of the valley, Lillie was sure that if they had not been named after her, she had been named after them. Every morning Leonard Mack departed the brownstone for his liquor business, stopping first at a shoe cleaner's stand near the corner for his daily shoe polishing. Everything about him, not merely his boots, was polished. When he died—too soon—Lillie was certain she would never laugh again.

It was a characteristically German-American Jewish home in which she matured, a home in which two languages were spoken, not to mention the language of the heart. In 1889 a third language was attempted—French—when the family traveled abroad and visited the Paris Exposition. There, Lillie was introduced to French art and architecture, history and language, and these interests too she would one day share with her daughter.

In due course Lillie was enrolled in Normal College, an institution that specialized in the training of teachers and would eventually be renamed Hunter College. My mother learned much at college, from which she graduated in 1890, but not the art of teaching school. She tried it for one day, developed a violent headache, and decided never to return to the classroom. (She did learn many other arts that, gathered together, pointed her way to humor and good sense, to what was once called loving-kindness, and especially to wisdom.)

Lillie Mack's new life as wife and mother began

with the new century. She had met her future husband at a neighborhood bowling club. Good-looking, mustachioed, and nearly ten years her senior, Moses R. Stern must have attracted her immediately. When she learned that the R. stood for Roland, a middle name he adopted himself, it intensified her regard. His choice to be the namesake of the legendary knight surely reflected a romantic imagination. Her only regret was that her father could not know the man she would marry.

Their engagement was announced at Thanksgiving dinner on 126th Street, the courtship lasted some six months, and on June 9, 1902, the marriage was solemnized by Rabbi Gustave Gottheil of Congregation Emanu-El. The wedding was briefly described in a newspaper article Lillie must have clipped and kept: The couple were married in "one of the private salons in the Hotel Savoy"; the bride, given away by her twin brother, "wore a gown of white silk crepe over silk trimmed with lace and a tulle veil fastened with orange blossoms." She carried a prayer book, and her ornaments included a pendant of diamonds and a collarette of pearls, all of which I now possess. "A wedding breakfast for relatives followed the ceremony."

Twenty-eight years of compatible marriage also followed the ceremony. My father hailed from a family and background similar to my mother's. They too had originated in Germany and settled, not in Cincinnati, but in another colony of German-Jewish émigrés planted in Hartford, Connecticut. There, Moe Stern was born in 1861, at the beginning of the Civil War. One of a large family, which included two sets of twins, he never lost his Yankee accent or his love of fun or his independent spirit. As a child he played hookey from Sabbath School to march in a parade and raise his voice in chanting "Onward, Christian Soldiers." That incident was a sign, not of deviation from the Jewish faith, but of prankish independence. When he matured, my father moved to New York to seek his fortune and, like my grandfather, opened a liquor business. The Stern business, however, was more specialized than the Mack version. My father restricted his operations to vermouth and advertised them with a card that read "Something to learn—Buy your vermouth from M. R. Stern." When the Volstead Act and Prohibition changed the face of the country, the vermouth specialist was forced to change the nature of his business, and he turned to bakers' supplies. One of my greatest joys was being taken by him to his huge rooms far west on 57th Street, where bottles and jars of colored liquids and solids fascinated me, and the agility of his secretary at typewriter keys filled me with admiration.

After a brief period when my parents lived in my grandmother's house on 126th Street, they moved to the apartment building that had been erected at the corner of Lenox Avenue—No. 101. My brother, Leonard Mack Stern, was born in April 1903, and Moses R. Stern immediately changed the name of his business to M. R. Stern & Son, although Leonard would never be a part of it. He must have been the center of his parents' attention during his first nine years, their pride and heir. His uncle ran a set of trains on the top floor of the brownstone at No. 133, where Leonard played. He spoke German before he spoke English, but as soon as he entered school he forgot the German language. Leonard was soon prepared to be a second-generation American. He would be less prepared to live with a baby sister. Nonetheless, on

July 1, 1912, when Leonard was nine, that baby sister was born.

LEONA

Although Louisa basked in the admiration of her young students at the Cherry Street charity school, that was not sufficient to make up for the deficiencies of her personal life. These came to a sudden climax when her beloved father, Leon Dreyfus, tragically suffered a sudden and massive heart attack and died, on October 5, 1898. Louisa would be twenty-nine on her next birthday, and in the eyes of the world and in her own eyes she was facing the end of youth, the end of opportunity. The marriages of her friends and the births of their children reminded her all too sharply of her own single state. Women who did not marry before they reached the age of thirty were doomed to spinsterhood. Louisa's flirtations had not and did not seem to be leading to the permanent relationship expected of all women.

In February 1902, still beautiful but increasingly hopeless, Louisa attended yet another engagement reception for a close friend, though such joyous occasions were becoming more and more painful to her. She had been invited by relatives in New Orleans to attend the approaching Mardi Gras, and she looked forward eagerly to that and the opportunities it might offer. Meanwhile, at her friend's engagement, she was introduced to a young German, a friend of the groom-to-be. Adolph Rostenberg was completely smitten, as he would later confess, by Louisa's "cherry eyes." A young physician, he had been in America only two years. He was obviously younger than Louisa, and she paid him but little attention. When he asked if she would see him soon again and tried to arrange a meeting, she hesitated, mentioning her forthcoming visit to New Orleans. The possibilities of Mardi Gras and a return to the scene of her early conquests eclipsed the attractions of a German physician far younger than she. Adolph Rostenberg could wait.

Her stay in New Orleans during the 1902 Mardi Gras is vividly described in her letters to her mother. The balls and masques, the parades and galas are all there—the almost frantic festivities of the city. Of particular interest is a letter in which she boasts of driving a horse and carriage along the Mississippi to the Godchaux Reserve Plantation, with its molasses and sugar refineries. "I drove the entire nine miles. They thought my driving a little reckless."

Louisa could not help comparing the city in which she had grown up to the far less provincial Crescent City of 1902. At carnival balls or operatic performances she compared also her gallant escorts with her past beaux and arrived at the sad conclusion: "The charm of the Northern woman does not appeal to the grace of the Southern man." The Mardi Gras interlude ended with a visit to a clairvoyant, who assured Miss Dreyfus that she would marry "a man of title" and bear him four children.

By the spring of 1902 Miss Dreyfus was back in New York. The February engagement reception where she had first met Dr. Adolph Rostenberg culminated in May in a wedding ceremony, and once again he was there—in truth "a man of title."

Six years younger than Louisa, he hailed from Königsberg, East Prussia. A mass of curly blond hair crowned his thin pale face, and through his unframed spectacles he gazed worshipfully at the charming, flirtatious Southern belle. Dr. Rostenberg was eager to impart his short life history to her, and, an attentive listener, Miss Dreyfus learned that, after studying at the Königsberg Gymnasium, Adolph had taken a medical degree at the University of Leipzig in 1899, serving the same year as resident physician at a sanitarium for high-strung young ladies in Bad Nauheim. Many of his patients were Americans, who filled his head with the golden prospects of a golden America. Ready to elude the German military draft and even readier to seek his gilded American future, Adolph sailed in May 1900 for the New World.

Although he had come to America many years later than the Mack and Dreyfus clans, his reasons for emigrating were almost identical. He soon settled in a German community of the Bronx known as Melrose Village, where the main thoroughfare, Courtlandt Avenue, was dubbed Dutch Broadway. Not long after, he opened an office close by, at 552 East 163rd Street. It was from Melrose Village in May 1902 that Dr. Rostenberg journeyed to Manhattan to attend the wedding of the couple at whose engagement party he had first glimpsed Louisa Dreyfus. There, to his great delight, the woman who had intrigued him was present again, now resplendent in the role of maid of honor. This time he would not let her escape.

With the Mardi Gras experience fresh in her mind, Louisa allowed her initial reluctance to melt away. The courtship began, and with it a series of courting letters from Dr. Rostenberg dated between June 4 and August 27, 1902. The first of the letters is addressed to "Dear Miss Dreyfuss," the surname misspelled, and it is signed, "Sincerely, Dr. Rostenberg." The last is addressed to "My dearest Louisa!" and signed "Your always devoted Adolph." Actually it took only eleven days for the transition to be made from "Dear Miss Dreyfuss" to "My darling good little comrade." By July it was "My best dearest Louisa!" and by August, "My dearest Darling!" One of the letters is addressed to "My dearest Uxor! [wife]."

The wedding, on December 25, 1902, was held at the bride's home, on West 111th Street, not far from the Mack-Stern home, in Harlem. Dr. Kaufmann Kohler performed the ceremony. After a four-day wedding trip to Lakewood, New Jersey, the couple set up house on Courtlandt Avenue. Four months later Louisa suffered a miscarriage. A year after, she gave birth to a frail infant boy who died several weeks later. Louisa was desperate. Could she do nothing right?

In September 1905 joy pervaded the home of Dr. and Mrs. Adolph Rostenberg with the birth of a healthy son, Adolph, Jr. Louisa took infinite delight in her little boy, devoting an entire Baby Book to his early development. The prediction of the New Orleans clairvoyant was finally fulfilled in December 1908, when baby Leona, named after her grandfather Leon, was born.

The New Orleans seer had not predicted that Leona would remain very small. I recall standing on Washington Avenue in the Bronx, gazing at the house where I was born. I was holding on lightly to Gertrude, my father's nurse-secretary, who took care of me between office hours. As usual, she was flirting with Joe Connelly, the grocer's clerk. I was dressed in a blue chinchilla coat lined in red, with blue leggings and a red cap pulled over my ears. I gazed longingly at our house, which I knew was warm and snug. It looked like a large bird, with black shutters that clacked in the wind, a red and white façade resembling the breast of a bird, and a tall black gate.

At home I spent much of my time in my large bedroom, where I played with my dolls and looked at the picture books I kept in a little stand. My tranquil life was disturbed only by my brother, who planned my swift demise by gagging me when I was sleeping and tying me to the bedpost, or triple-daring me to dip my pinky finger into boiling water.

No wonder I was an extremely shy child—a condition exacerbated by my having to wear eyeglasses, unlike any of my contemporaries. My shyness worried my social-minded mother. Nonetheless, I enjoyed kindergarten the following year. I loved the cutouts, pasting and drawing. Once in P.S. 28 I became addicted to reading and writing, learning to spell big words. With my mother, I visited the library next door and selected books relating to history and the presidents of the United States. For my ninth birthday I received a complete set of the *Little Women* series, by Louisa May Alcott, which I devoured. I resented my mother's efforts to take me to any social event but was finally compelled to attend a dancing class. I was then ten but, because of my small stature, looked like an eight-year-old. I talked to few children, though I remembered a very outgoing girl named Madeleine. I did not see her outside dancing class, since she lived in distant Manhattan and I lived in the Bronx.

The following year my mother told me, "Daddy and I have wonderful news. We are moving into a castle. I will show it to you next week." And so we walked along Tremont Avenue over the big intersection at Webster and up the hill to the Grand Concourse. At 179th Street we turned down the hill to a house at the corner of Creston Avenue. My mother looked at me expectantly. "This is your new home, darling—your castle." I was vastly disappointed. There were no knights and ladies, no joustings, no white chargers. "You exaggerate," I exploded. My mother laughed and took me inside to the house that would be my home for fifty years.

MADELEINE

Leonard's baby sister, Madeleine, born in 1912, was quick to question her presence, if not in the world, in one small part of it. Legend has it that after the family settled at a New Jersey beach resort for summer vacation in 1914, Madeleine, age two, piped up with "Why I here?" Probably my first intelligible sentence, the question indicated not only awareness of a strange landscape, but what is known as an inquiring mind.

A bit later, my inquiring mind induced me to physical action. On a train ride with my parents, I was somehow intrigued by the man seated directly in front of us. I apparently wished to investigate the nature of his head, since I reached over and removed his hat. The uncovered area was completely bald. My researches into the strange and unexplored had begun.

The photograph that parallels the one of Leona was taken when I was three. Like Leona's, it depicts a little child, if not actually reading, then appearing to read. And like Leona, I am pondering the information I have acquired from the news. Like my query, "Why I here?", like my investigation of a bald head, this picture is a prelude. It is a prologue to a life devoted to reading, to print, to books—just as Leona's likeness is. Inevitably, those two portraits were to come together.

By the age of four, I was still pretending to read.

Seated on a porch in the country, I bent my head over a book, only to be interrupted in my performance by a passing visitor's devastating remark: "Little girl, you are holding that book upside down!"

Kindergarten and first grade at P.S. 128 soon converted my pretense into reality. Learning to read, learning to love books, was a seminal part of my life and started me growing together with those who shared that love.

What do I remember of those early years? Certainly nothing of World War I and its aftermath. Rather, the wholesome, comforting smell of library paste in kindergarten, where we made cutouts and glued them together. Rather, the adventure of riding the subway with my father, who would call out to me the first and last letters of words in the ads overhead and watch as I located the fitting word. What a lovely game that was. And the snowy winters on a sled pulled by my big brother. And walking hand in hand with my mother to market—sawdust on the floor—for groceries in barrels or arrowroot cookies in open tins. And later in the street with my companions—mostly boys—fishing for coins through subway gratings with sticks tipped with slightly chewed gum.

Dicky Loeb, three years my senior, who lived above us in the apartment house, initiated two adventures of my childhood that have been told in *Old Books, Rare Friends*. They were sufficiently important to merit becoming twice-told tales, and so I raise the curtain once again on those dramas of my youth.

With the first fall of snow, Dicky would suggest that we offer our services as snow shovelers. We were hired at a nearby brownstone by a woman, dressed in red, who promised to pay us thirty-five cents to clean her areaway. We worked hard for an hour and then went to claim our wages. This time a woman in blue came to the door, looked us and the areaway over, and announced, "I never hired you to shovel." This was probably my first confrontation with evil. I could not comprehend it. When I decided that the lady had planned it all along and changed her outfit to pretend a different identity, Dicky and I conferred together and came up with a solution: "Let's shovel it all back again." It took us another hour, but we did. We were never paid, but justice had been served.

Dicky and I competed too for the summer job of

superintending Mr. Joseph's newsstand at our corner. "The job will go to the one who gets here at seven A.M.," Mr. Joseph announced, and since Dicky loved to sleep late, I won. During the summer mornings, I minded the stand, sometimes fetching papers from the local *Times* office, making change, becoming familiar with the vast variety of newspapers—sporting papers and financial papers, story papers and racing papers, papers in Yiddish and papers in Italian, papers from Ireland and from Germany. The smell of newsprint joined the smell of library paste in my olfactory memory, neither ever to be forgotten. To crown that glorious summer, a patron once gave me a ten-cent tip for handing him a two-cent paper, and so made me an optimist forever.

My mother did not omit the social graces even as she encouraged me to pursue my independence. Dancing class was a must in those days, and I attended in the tutu she had sewed for me. I remember nothing at all of the steps we learned or tried to learn, but I do remember a hushed conversation with another pupil on the subject of childbirth. It was my triumph to be able to inform him that the stork had absolutely nothing to do with the process. I was not sure what did have to do with it, but I knew for sure that the stork was not responsible. And there too, in dancing class, where there were children of all ages, from about five to ten, I met another pupil as uninterested in dancing steps as I, a shy girl about three years my senior. She did not pay me much attention, but I noticed and remembered that she always carried a book with her. I remember also that her first name was Leona.

When I was about eight or nine, my father told me a story that intrigued me. Everyone, he said, everyone in the whole wide world had a double somewhere, though no one knew exactly where. At that time, being very literal-minded, I thought of my double as a twin who would look precisely like me, act as I did, think exactly as I did. For a long time I wondered if ever and where and when I would locate the duplicate of myself who would know my thoughts and be part of me.

The possibility of such a wondrous encounter came back to me when, in the early 1920s, my parents informed me that we were to move from Harlem and live farther downtown. At first I was disturbed by the thought of moving. I loved walking on 125th Street, visiting a glassblower's establishment, being taken to the Apollo Theatre for a vaudeville performance, watching bonfires on Lenox Avenue on Election Eve, eating chocolate pastries at Karoly's Café, listening, as I fell asleep at night, to the trolley cars a block away. I could not see any reason for moving away from all this, but apparently my parents did, and so, when I was ten or eleven, the move was made, and I consoled myself with the thought that perhaps in our new location I would find my double.

No double manifested itself at 317 West 99th Street. Nonetheless, the move to the foot of a short steep hill between West End Avenue and Riverside Drive—one window overlooking the lordly Hudson—brought many changes into my life and shaped the background for my maturity.

With the new location, of course, came a new school. P.S. 93 was also known as Joan of Arc Junior High School. Its reputation was such that its principal, Laura Charlton, boasted that if she had the space she could empty all the private schools of New York. There I came to know and love my English teacher, Grace

Macdonald, who taught us by reading poetry aloud, transporting us to the empyrean. There too I met Shirley and Helen. They were not my doubles by any stretch of the imagination, but they were my friends, with whom I played and studied, acted and went to movies and theaters, wrote verses and talked into the wee hours. Shirley was petite and vivacious; Helen more solid in appearance, more commanding in presence. Both were in love with laughter, in love with books, in search of adventure. When we were not making up stories, we were reading them; when we were not giggling, we were chattering; when we were not versifying, we were showing off. We wrote at least one poem daily. Above all, we were all romancing, pretending to romance, looking for romance.

One summer Shirley and I applied for a course in prosody at Columbia University, were accepted despite our knee socks and middy blouses, and survived the serious literary criticism of Professor Hoxie Fairchild. Another summer—that of 1925—I spent in Europe.

My mother's sister, my Aunt Annie, had arranged to go abroad with two friends, schoolteachers. They had planned a comprehensive two-month tour, covering the European highlights but concentrating on Scandinavia. My parents thought that their twelve-year-old daughter, soon to be thirteen, would appreciate such an adventure and therefore proposed a choice to me: "Four summers in camp or this one summer in Europe." How could I have known that my profession of rare books would necessitate annual trips abroad for most of my life? Just now the lure of bringing the map of Europe to life, of seeing foreign lands and speaking with their people, surmounted the thought of swimming in a Maine lake or hiking through Maine woods. I chose Europe without any hesitation.

A leather-bound octavo tells the story of that adventure—or at least part of the story. *My Trip Abroad* includes a hundred pages of cramped script describing my reactions to Sweden, Norway and Denmark, Holland and Belgium, France and England. If those reactions also encapsulate the detailed data imparted by a succession of enthusiastic guides, that was because I listened carefully and scooped up much information and misinformation. If the language is sesquipedalian, it is because I was obviously in love with words and determined never to use a short one if

I could think up a long one. And if the diary lacks any overt mention of homesickness, it is because the traveler, just entering her teens, had never before been separated from her parents and was trying to counteract a desperate loneliness with a determination to expand her horizons.

Being even then a bit more rigid than I should have been, I decided that an album entitled *My Trip Abroad* should contain only the trip abroad and not the trans-Atlantic trip. Hence the hundred pages of *My Trip Abroad* are preceded by nineteen separate, unbound pages recording the voyage aboard the S.S *Stockholm*. The best way to follow the homesick child between the day of departure, June 30, 1925, and her return in September aboard the Royal Mail steamship *Orca* is to quote a few diary excerpts:

July 11, 1925. GOTHENBURG, SWEDEN. *We gained entrance to the Gothenburg Art Museum, which contains treasures valued over the entire universe. My favorite painting reveals a hay mound, casting its shadow over the grasses of spring. Hens and ducks play in the warm sunshine, and such peace seems to rest upon the scene that one would love to lie there, hidden in the leaves. I have already secured a postal copy of this wondrous landscape painted by Johan Krouther in 1884.*

Aug. 14, 1925. PARIS, FRANCE. *If I were to state all the marvelous relics which we have seen to-day, I would write until doomsday, so I shall cease, saying that no one who has not seen, can conceive of the glories offered to the Royal family in bygone years, and likewise of the disasters which befell them. After our strenuous day, we are content to retire at an early hour, and we shall now recline in our comfortable chambers.*

Aug. 24, 1925. LONDON, ENGLAND. . . . *We drove to Stoke Poges church, where Thomas Gray wrote his beautiful Elegy. No one but one immortal could describe this peaceful spot where lie those "once pregnant with celestial fire," and none could have made this*

*quiet churchyard as holy a place as did he! . . .
I cannot say how much more this solemn Elegy
means to me than it did previously.*

*We departed and drove to Eton College,
which is supported by pillars of romance and
which will be so until the end of time. All over
the desks, walls and tables are carved the names
of those who were illustrious when frequenting
this college. We saw Shelley's name carved by
himself . . . likewise Thomas Gray's . . . and
many other well-known titles. . . .*

*[At Windsor Castle] we saw the door
through which Anne Boleyn was led to her execution, and the results of many other most
interesting occurrences.*

Aug. 25, 1925. LONDON, ENGLAND. *Another day of marvels has been experienced by
us, for we saw the sights of the fine old city of
London. We boarded the same charabanc,
and, accompanied by our guide, we visited the
renowned Tower of London! After being led
through the dungeons, where many a tear has*

been shed in vain, we visited the exhibitions of arms and armour, and likewise were shown some instruments of torture. We then climbed to the room containing the Crown Jewels! Not only the Cullinan, or the largest diamond in the world, but also such jewels as I have never seen before!

Aug. 29, 1925. EN ROUTE. ON S.S. "Orca." Never can a trip be more wondrous than that of this beautiful season, and presently, as we speed to "my native land," I am impatient to relate the experiences which have befallen us.

The summer of 1925 had been momentous for me. The language in which I recorded it, stilted and hyperbolic though it was, gives glimpses of my exposure to worlds all new to me. Once home, however, my life resumed its course, and much that had begun in Harlem proceeded without interruption. I had attended Sunday School before our move, and I continued to do so after it.

I realize now that my attendance there was the primary link in the chain that would lead me to my so-called double. Only gradually would I come to understand that my father's use of the word *double* was an oversimplification for a child. There were no doubles. But there were counterparts; there were friends, friends in depth. When my parents enrolled me in Temple Emanu-El's Sunday School, they set me in her direction. Had I not gone to Sunday School, I think now I would never have met her. Not that she was there. No, it would still be several years before we actually met. But I was on the way.

I took Sunday School fairly seriously. We studied Jewish history with our teacher, attended a few services given by the rabbi, Dr. Enelow, and we learned a little Hebrew. If we were occasionally exposed to other-worldliness, there was still ample worldliness displayed by pupils who discussed their clothes from De Pinna and their big sisters' engagement rings from Tiffany. I was a member of the last class to be confirmed from Temple Emanu-El while it was still located in a Moorish temple at 43rd Street and Fifth Avenue, and the Confirmation Service on Monday morning, June 6, 1927, was memorable, especially since I still have a copy of the program.

After the entrance of the Confirmation Class, tributes were paid to the Torah and to Judaism, its doctrines and teachers, its traditions and practices, its virtues and its Messianic hope. The Response to the prayers of Messianic hope was sung by the choir: "For as the earth bringeth forth her growth, And as the garden causeth things sown to bring forth; So the Lord God will cause victory and glory to spring forth before all the nations." This was an appropriate Response in the year 1927, before World War II and the Holocaust. At that Confirmation Service I had the honor of delivering the Opening Prayer, and the Confirmation sermon was given by Dr. Nathan Krass, the Confirmation Resolves by Dr. H. G. Enelow. The service closed with the singing of *En Kelohenu* and with the Benediction.

It had been preceded by another service, which included the awarding of prizes. The Lewis May medal for Jewish history and the Gustave Gottheil medal for Hebrew were granted on the basis of a long written test. The tests were signed pseudonymously by the pupils, and I took the name of Joan of Arc, in tribute to my junior high school. Joan of Arc won both medals. My parents, who had been married by Gustave Gottheil, must have been gratified when I was awarded the medal in his name.

Another who was especially gratified was one of my Sunday School teachers, Miss Henrietta Solomon, who presented me with a psalter inscribed to "dear little Madeleine Stern." Henrietta Solomon happened to be an acquaintance of Leona's mother. She had a project in preparation that, within a few years, would bring together those two counterparts, Madeleine and Leona.

Meanwhile, like my Sunday School attendance, my piano lessons, begun in Harlem, continued. Professor Frank was probably more bored than tolerant with a pupil who lacked all musical talent. At least, after our move to 99th Street, I no longer donned my Indian pants and headgear when he arrived for lessons. That eccentricity discarded, I now appeared at the piano stool decorously enough in my middy blouse and navy skirt. Seated before our upright Knabe—a must in most middle-class homes at the time—I went through the motions, reading the notes facilely enough but usually rushing through the banalities of a "Pizzicato" or the intricacies of a "Moonlight Sonata." My music lessons were, to put it kindly, unproductive. One day Leona's very musical father would admonish me: "Madeleine, if you really loved music, you would stop playing."

Some time after my return from my "wondrous" trip abroad in 1925, my private French lessons began. In these I demonstrated more ability than at the piano. My teacher, Monsieur André Paul, was an enthusiast. We sat side by side at my desk and, insisting upon speaking French only, he told me about the Alliance Française, the philosophy of Jean Jaures, the political movements of postwar France. It was a big intellectual dose for a teenager, especially in a foreign language. But besides achieving a smattering of French, I felt a stimulation and a desire to learn more, not only about the country's language, but about its history. When he left, Monsieur Paul invariably added to his *"Au revoir, Mademoiselle,"* the admonition: *"Etudiez bien."*

Mademoiselle was "étudier-ing"—studying— also at Hunter High School. A heavy program of solid subjects there included French and Latin, English, mathematics and history. We took *dictée* from Miss Dalton in French; solved geometric problems under the guidance of Miss Cromack, whom we dubbed "Lizzy Poip" (for "perpendicular"); followed the historical investigations of Miss Ver Planck; journeyed to ancient Rome with Miss Corrigan; and heard the magical phrases of Shelley and Keats from the lips of Miss Sebring, a reimbodiment of "my" Miss Macdonald. Our teachers' titles were invariably "Miss." There was no man in sight among students or faculty at Hunter High.

We could, and did, vary the hours of study as well as the gender limitations at theater and the movies. With Helen, who had moved with me to Hunter High from Joan of Arc, and with Shirley, who had chosen Wadleigh High instead, we saw Rostand's unforgettable romance *Cyrano de Bergerac* on the Broadway stage. John Gilbert and Greta Garbo were our favorite movie stars, and we sat through *Flesh and the Devil* at least five times. As a tribute to her special hero, Helen sent to Mr. Gilbert the collected works of Henrik Ibsen.

We read Ibsen, especially after we had seen Eva Le Gallienne perform *The Master Builder* at the Civic Repertory Theatre on 14th Street. But we also read and reread Charlotte Brontë's *Jane Eyre,* Emily Brontë's *Wuthering Heights,* Louisa May Alcott's *Little Women,* not to mention the mysteries detected by Sherlock Holmes.

We were all in those days feasting on a life of study and learning, savoring new concepts, formulating new thoughts, seeking new adventures. In the midst of this intellectual banquet, my father's illness cast a dark shadow. He had suffered a mild stroke around the time we moved from Harlem, and now he suffered others in a frightening succession. He would die of one in 1930. Meanwhile he had been forced to retire from business, and he spent his hours trying to retrieve the use of his leg muscles, getting fresh air on the roof, and reading. He read all the books he had missed in his youth. He plowed through whole sets of Walter Scott and Thackeray. He looked on, while the family lived on. My mother made our home and participated actively in all our endeavors. My brother married and left the household. I continued my studies, preparing now for college, continued my friendship with Helen and Shirley, continued my egocentric life.

I had little time or inclination in those days to look back; my thoughts were hinged to the future. And had I looked back, I would never have been able to assess the most important experience in my life thus far. Indeed, I would have dismissed that experience as incidental and insignificant. It was not my schooling, not my friendship with Helen and Shirley, not the piano and French lessons, not my trip abroad, not the plays I had seen—none of these. The most important experience in my life had been, it would turn out, my attendance at Sunday School. After Confirmation, my mother had held open house. We were especially honored that day when both the rabbis came to our home to offer their congratulations to the girl who had won the Lewis May and the Gustave Gottheil medals. My parents must have been very proud. I too was proud. Ironically, however, I was completely unaware that my days at Sunday School had paved the way for the most important meeting of my life.

That meeting, still a few years off, would lead eventually to the friendship that was to define and illuminate my life. Meanwhile, college lay ahead, and the writing of my first published book. Only after all that would my father's story of the world's doubles be confirmed for me.

I was admitted to Barnard. In 1929 I became a freshman there—a February freshman, and hence a bit out of things, since most had entered in the fall. This, coupled with the fact that none of my friends from Joan of Arc or Hunter was with me, made me feel displaced for a time. I missed Helen and Shirley. I even missed my teachers, although Hoxie Fairchild made up for that in a small way. When he saw me in the hall, he remembered my appearance in his summer course in prosody and called out, "Well! Welcome! You made it at last."

It took a while until I did feel welcome. Not only did I miss my friends, I watched as they began pairing off with the young men whom they would eventually marry. I went through a series of beaux, but none of them—they knew and I knew—seemed the companion for life each of us sought. Barnard had its compensations in a course on Shakespeare and another on Chaucer, but more and more I felt like the Cheese in the Farmer in the Dell. The Farmer would take his Wife and the Wife would take the Child, but the Cheese would inevitably stand alone, as I seemed to be doing. Eventually I would write a novel called *We Are Taken* based on that very theme. But just now, during my first year at Barnard, an event occurred that would reshape my world. I think I had been unconsciously preparing for it all my life.

External conditions also prepared me. My own loneliness at observing my friends pairing off was accompanied by the national Depression. As a result of the prolonged economic crisis, any job, any means of earning pocket money, not to mention a living, seemed unattainable. It was true that I had been awarded a Regents Scholarship—$100 a year for the four college years—and that equaled twenty-five percent of the tuition. And as for pocket money, the Dean of Barnard offered thirty-five cents an hour for walking her dogs—a most desirable job that, of course, was no longer available.

Into this bleak picture, while I was a Barnard freshman, entered the welcome image of my former Sunday School teacher, Miss Henrietta Solomon. She telephoned one day and asked if I would be interested in teaching at the Sabbath School sponsored by Temple Emanu-El. She was now its director, she explained, and she knew that my years at Sunday School had well prepared me for such an assignment. Her niece was one of the teachers. "And," she added, "our staff also includes a young woman, a senior at New York University, the daughter of a friend of mine. You may know her—her name is Leona Rostenberg." The name rang a distant bell. At the moment I was far more interested in the materialistic aspects of the proposed job. Miss Solomon quickly satisfied me. "You would be teaching on Saturday mornings, and the pay would be two-fifty a morning."

Manna had fallen upon me from heaven. I was to teach the older pupils, and I quickly assembled a pile of index cards upon which I wrote the salient points of biblical history, remembered from my Emanu-El days or researched in a text entitled *Outlines of Jewish History.* My years at Sunday School had more than prepared me for this moment; they had qualified me. In September 1929 I appeared with my sheaf of notes and my package of index cards at the beautiful building on 15th Street and Second Avenue known as the Hebrew Technical School for Girls.

Both girls and boys appeared there on Saturdays for instruction in Jewish history. I soon realized that I was taking the assignment of teaching them far more seriously than anyone else. Miss Solomon's niece spent a good portion of the morning looking for bargains at nearby Klein's on the Square; Miss Solomon herself could be found most of the time in a small office where she made all her personal social telephone calls, and Leona Rostenberg, to whom I was introduced, seemed to be teaching her eight-year-old students less Jewish history than the European history she had learned at New York University.

She was a very short young woman, not more than four feet ten. She was vibrantly alive, quite loquacious, and she seemed to notice everything. Yet she held herself to herself. She was a senior and I a mere freshman. To compensate for the difference, I decided she was less intellectual than I. I even had the audacity to describe her in a telephone conversation with a friend, but within her hearing, as "Lots of fun, but no intellect." In the many decades of our growing

and being together, she would never forget that remark, raising her eyebrows as she laughingly repeated
it. We spent as much time laughing together as talking, eating ice cream cones while our classes were
having Hebrew lessons. Our friendship, if such it
could be called, was on the light side. After all, she
was still a senior and I was still a freshman. It was not
yet time for close friendship. But we had met.

If our friendship did not endure at the time, neither did the school. As Leona's pupil Eddie put it, when
she asked if he would return next year, "Nah, we don't
learn nuttin here." It so happened that he could not
have returned anyway. The school closed the next year,
our salaries vanished, and our friendship faded.

Fortunately for me, an even better paying proposal was offered by one of my Barnard professors,
Charles Baldwin, who sported a black cape most of
the time. The professor had met aboard ship the
charming Countess Colloredo-Mansfield, an American, a former Iselin, now married to an Austrian
count. The countess had confided to the English professor that she would like to be tutored in the art of
versification, since her psychiatrist had suggested that

she write poetry about mimosa. Charles Baldwin thought of me in this connection. After all, had I not taken a course in prosody years ago? Did I not produce poems at the rate of one a day? The countess requested a one-hour lesson each week, for which she would be happy to pay three dollars. The countess thus provided me with an income during most of my college years. I, in turn, taking my work with high seriousness, taught her the secrets of rhyme and rhythm, meter and verse forms, and doubtless provided her too with well-disguised amusement. On the wings of Pegasus but clad in a gingham dress, I arrived at her elaborate establishment in New York and carried her to poetic heights. Under my tutelage the Countess Colloredo-Mansfield not only ventured beyond the confines of mimosa but left me a three-dollar check even when she could not appear for a lesson.

My friends were by now seriously paired off—Helen deeply in love with handsome Raymond, dubbed "Hidalgo" for his striking good looks; Shirley bewitched at first by poetic David, but turning later to the more manly Alvin. I "dated" a succession of young men, none of whom aroused either my passion or my intellectual interest. For gratification of that interest I turned to my studies. There, during my last two years, I was offered what was called an honors course in English literature based upon the Oxford version. Its goal was intellectual expansion through intellectual independence. I could audit any course I wished but was not required to attend any classes or take any examinations until just before graduation. At that time I was given a nine-hour written examination, covering not only English literature but English philology, and a lengthy oral examination, at which I was questioned by the entire English faculty. Seated around a long table, they pelted me with questions, while I, wearing a nondescript dress topped by what I thought a jaunty white beret, provided interminable answers. We plodded through the centuries from Beowulf to Thomas Hardy, from the complexities of English syntax to the future of *shall* and *will*. In addition to all this, I was required to submit a paper on a chosen subject, and I prepared one on the Shakespeare play in which I was then most interested, *The Tempest*. On June 1, 1932, I received my B.A. degree, with honors in English, at the commencement ceremony held in Columbia University's South Court.

I had tested my intellectual independence and reveled in it. But in June 1932 the only career I could hope to enter was teaching, teaching not in the halls of academe but in New York's public school system. There were three reasons for such a severe limitation: I was a woman and I was a Jew. Whether anti-feminism or anti-Semitism was overt or covert, it existed and usually prevailed. In addition, I had graduated from college in the midst of the Great Depression.

In order to qualify for a teaching post in New York City's high schools in 1932, the applicant was required to have a master's degree. In 1933 I began studying for my master's at Columbia. There, under the guidance of my friend, the elegant Professor Charles Baldwin, I wrote my master's essay on the role of Mary Magdalene in medieval literature. The essay had a dramatic history of its own. Following the custom of the time, I submitted my original and only copy to the English Department for retyping, shortly to be informed that two-thirds of it had inexplicably disappeared from the office. One third was on hand, retyped. Fortunately, my investigations of

Mary Magdalene had been so voluminous that the extant third was accepted in lieu of the whole, and my degree was granted.

Before I became a master, I spent a summer weekend, with my friend Helen and her friend Raymond, at an adult camp in Pennsylvania known as Log Tavern. In the early 1930s adult camps were as popular among young people as Elderhostels are today among senior citizens. Performances, given in the evenings, ranged from experiments in mesmerism to vocal auditions and stage plays. But it was primarily with dating or mating in view that young couples and singles flocked to adult camps. Log Tavern, like most of them, even had its own newspaper. Wandering one day into the newspaper office with Helen, I encountered a young woman editing with a blue pencil. We introduced ourselves, "I am Lucy Bender," she said, and when she heard my name she commented, "I know about you. You know Leona Rostenberg, and Leona is my best friend. How about getting together?" It was probably the most important question I had ever been asked. It was the question that would give me my future.

LEONA

Madeleine's future—like mine—was shaped in large measure by the past. Much of mine was centered in the house on the hill to which we had moved in the spring of 1918, before I was ten.

Although the Bronx "castle" lacked tower and turret, it contained fourteen large rooms and twenty-one closets—ample for play and study. On my second day in my new home I was seated on the windowseat of the dining room, gazing wistfully at two of my neighbors, girls my own age, skipping rope. I longed to participate, but shyness prevented me. Finally, the taller of the two called in a very superior voice, "Come out, little girl, and join us." I was immediately interrogated about whether I skipped rope. When I said no, I was eyed superciliously. The next question—"What class are you in, little girl?"—put me in a superior position since I was in a higher class than my inquisitor. "4B," I pronounced with authority. My interrogator appeared stunned. I was immediately accepted into the inner circle of rope jumpers. I had outwitted them scholastically.

As time passed, I gained a few friends and lost some of my shyness. When, in 1922, my father went to Berlin to become acquainted with the newest strides in dermatology, his family followed two months later. I was forced to miss my public school graduation ceremony. My disappointment was somewhat assuaged by the principal's presentation to me of *Lights to Literature*. This priceless gift accompanied me to Europe and was shown to my father as soon as he greeted us at Cuxhaven.

A small ledger distributed by the Hamburg-America Line briefly describes my reactions to a multitude of German castles, thrones, gardens, and mausoleums. Unlike Madeleine's ecstatic and detailed account of the Gothenburg Museum and the "wondrous" glories of France and England, my diary is a brief statistical survey of my itinerary and my purchases in Berlin, Munich, and Oberammergau, where I saw the Passion Play. In spite of my concentration upon regal sites—palaces and their throne chairs, the royal regalia of crowns and scepters—my heart and my diary remained true to the land of the free and the home of the brave. The diary should have been bound in red, white, and blue.

Upon my return home I entered Evander Childs High School, where at first I felt quite lost. My official class included the school's baseball team, men of importance and self-importance. I was still a little girl wearing socks. During my sophomore year I met another small girl, with long blond curls and a winning smile. Her name was Lucy Bender. We shortly became fast friends, and I followed wherever she led. I liked where she led me—late afternoons in ice cream parlors, cutting classes for movies, long discussions about her future. She planned to be an actress or work in Hollywood.

Lucy was a very determined young lady. During her senior year but before she could graduate she gave up high school to work at Keith's Palace Theatre. She abandoned her education for the thrill of assisting the actress Beatrice Lillie. Her chief assignment consisted of holding the comedienne's costumes for quick changes. Nonetheless, Lucy now appeared as a superior being, part of the theatrical world. Before

Lucy served the great Bea Lillie, my mother decided to forge my future and sent me to camp, hoping to eradicate my shyness, rid me of my thralldom to Lucy, and at the same time acquaint me with proper children, that is, scions of German-Jewish households.

The camp she chose was Kearsage, on Lake Sebago in Naples, Maine. I had never been away from home alone. I had never traveled without my parents. I had met few of the proper German-Jewish children. At camp I discovered I was the only child who attended public school, the only child who lived in the Bronx, and the only child who had never heard of De Pinna, clothier to the proper children. I thought De Pinna was a wild animal or an island discovered by Captain Cook. Nevertheless, my social shortcomings intrigued the scions of the wealthy, and, as an anomaly, I was not only accepted but was extremely popular. In spite of my limitations at basketball and my inability to dive off the high dive, I was "Peanut," well loved and warmly befriended.

I recall that during a conversation with one of the junior campers, Teresa White, she mentioned some of her best friends. "Oh, you should meet my good friend Madeleine Stern. She goes to public school like you, but she's very smart and helps edit her school paper. You would like her." The name seemed vaguely familiar, but I dismissed it when the bugle blew for afternoon swimming. My years at camp served me well. I lost much of my shyness and I broadened my horizons.

Despite the influence of Kearsage, my foibles at Evander remained on my record, and when it came to college applications I was denied admission to Barnard College.

It was the fall of 1926. I felt alone and outcast. I had no school to attend, no program to follow. My relationship with Lucy was changing. She had moved to her own apartment and was busy working at a job or chasing boys. My parents did not push their "sensitive plant." They believed I would find myself. I finally registered for a few courses in history and English literature at Columbia University Extension, a division of the university that did not require credentials but did not grant degrees. At the end of the academic year I realized I was getting nowhere, and applied for admission to Washington Square College, the downtown branch of New York University. There, I majored in history. Although I basically disliked the college—it lacked the aroma of a college—I made a few friends and enjoyed my courses in English history, ancient civilization, and the Renaissance. I was fascinated by history. I became familiar with the Medicis of Florence, the guile of the Renaissance papacy, the Huguenot struggle in France. I was being prepared to dig and to recount. My interests were becoming focused.

In the summer of 1928 I went abroad with my mother. Aboard ship she bumped into two old acquaintances, Henrietta and Rebecca Solomon. As the shipboard friendship developed, Henrietta, the elder of the two sisters, asked whether I would be interested in teaching a class of children the annals of Judaism at Sabbath School. She added, "We pay quite well—two-fifty a morning." I was delighted at the prospect and immediately accepted, without a thought to my own qualifications or lack of them. "Fine," she said, "I'll get in touch with you in September."

Fortunately, Miss Solomon was unaware of my

deficiency in Jewish history. Like the children of most middle-class Jewish families at the time, I had been enrolled in the neighborhood Sunday School, sponsored by the Tremont Temple. My brother had also been enrolled. The rabbi, a family friend, phoned my mother shortly after, imploring her to do him a great favor. "Louisa, would you kindly remove your son from Sunday School? He is destroying the morale of the entire class. He arrives on skates, punches holes in paper wine glasses, and pays no attention at all to his teachers. He is disrupting all the other pupils." My brother was removed from Tremont Temple Sunday School. Alas! So too was I. Hence my knowledge of Jewish history was minimal, and I knew I would have to brush up on it for Miss Henrietta Solomon.

For the first year, Miss Solomon's niece, the Hebrew teacher, and I formed the faculty of the Sabbath School on 15th Street and Second Avenue. I added little to my eight-year-old pupils' knowledge of Jewish history, but I did add to their scant store of learning considerable information about Greek and Roman civilization and the ups and downs of British history. As I wrote in my diary, "Didn't know very much about the Bible so told my youngsters remarkable fantasies concerning mummies and obelisks." For better or worse, my courses at New York University provided me with substance for my Sabbath School teaching.

At the beginning of my second year there, Miss Solomon informed me that she had engaged a teacher who really knew Jewish history. The older pupils would be assigned to her. On the second Saturday of September in 1929 I was introduced to the new teacher, Madeleine Stern. She seemed slightly familiar to me—reserved and a bit aloof. It was true that she was teaching the older children, but since she was a mere freshman at Barnard, I knew she was younger than I. We had little to do with each other at first, although our classes came together at assembly. As a Barnard student, Madeleine continued to seem aloof. Gradually we did become friendlier, sharing ice cream cones and talking about college. My diary entry for February 8, 1930, comments: "Madeleine Stern's really nice and we've decided to manage the whole place." The immediate prospects of a closer relationship, however, were nipped in the bud when we were informed by Miss Solomon that the school would not open the next year. The Depression had caught religion too in its grip.

The June 11, 1930, entry in my diary reads: "Leona Rostenberg, Bachelor of Arts—reporting a great day in her life—oh, it was thrilling and so beautiful and I can scarcely realize I'm really through, commenced and finished. My heart leapt." For the next two years I vainly fought the persistent Depression by translating writings from the German that never achieved publication and by writing short stories that also remained in manuscript. In 1932 I again registered at Columbia University, this time at the Graduate School of Political Science. A return to academe was the only path available to the footloose Leona. I took courses in medieval and modern history under Lynn Thorndike and Carlton J. H. Hayes. In late January 1933, Professor Hayes confronted his class, stating, "Today President Hindenburg appointed Adolf Hitler Chancellor of Germany. The world will never be the same."

Very few in this country had Professor Hayes's prophetic insight. At the time, the full implication of his observation was neither heeded nor comprehended. The news that came to us out of Germany seemed to indicate civil strife between Nazis and Communists, although rumors of increasing anti-Semitism excited my German Jewish father to explosions about his ancestral land. Nonetheless, no one could have foretold the Holocaust that would follow. Most Americans had no intimations of such horror. Certainly I had none.

In June 1933, I received my master's degree from Columbia University and decided to go on and study for a doctorate. I continued to be sheltered from the upheavals of a rapidly changing world. I was not even aware that my own world would soon be transformed. That metamorphosis would be the outcome not of world events but of a simple occurrence at home: in the fall, I met Madeleine Stern again.

De L'Education Des Dames Pour La Conduite De L'Esprit Dans Les Sciences Et Dans Les Moeurs [On the Education of Women in matters concerning their spiritual and intellectual conduct]. François Poulain de La Barre, French, 1674

A feminist manifesto for self-searching women. The author, a seventeenth-century French philosopher, encourages women to resolve their problems, advocating for them an almost unlimited education and assuring them that no studies are beyond them. Bound in calf.

Acquired by the New York Public Library, 1951

Chapter Two

SELF-SEARCHING

LEONA

That meeting took place in September of 1933. On September 1 of that year I wrote in my diary: "This date means the beginning of a new year." The succeeding entries for September refer to my plans for graduate study, my friends and their infants, my readings, my writings, my dates, my hopes and my fears— but not to the meeting with Madeleine. That meeting had been accompanied by no trumpet fanfare. Nothing had occurred in its brief course to predict that it was freighted with destiny. Had I mentioned it in my diary, I would probably have written: "Met Madeleine Stern again—she's still good fun and she seems less aloof than before."

The setting of the meeting was the West 88th

Street home of Madeleine's friend from junior high school, Helen Keppler, who had accompanied her to Log Tavern, and its cast of characters included the quartet of Madeleine and Helen, Lucy Bender and myself. The only dramatic incident marking the afternoon was the toast we all made to the future, with brandy daringly served by our hostess. But the meeting—the re-meeting—had taken place. This time it would propel us, not only into a new year, but into a new life.

When I met Madeleine at Sabbath School, we had not been ready for such friendship. The Barnard freshman had been too immature and cocksure; the NYU senior had been too filled with self-doubt and lack of focus. Now we stood on more common ground. We had come together again at a climactic moment in our lives, when we were both seeking maturity and certainly both seeking to find ourselves, both groping for identity.

My own gropings are dramatically expressed in the pages of the diaries I kept during the late 1920s and early 1930s. Those diaries were the receptacles for my frustrations and my aspirations during the years before my professional interests and my emotional reactions were channeled. Besides recording my occasional domestic frictions and my visits with friends, the books I was reading, the nature of the men I encountered, my love of children and the plays I saw from the second balcony, the pages of my early diaries are reflections of a nature in perplexity and doubt, yearning to find herself. In a way, I could have been called—and Freud probably would have called me—a split personality.

Both my despair and my hope are encapsulated in a single sentence penned at the start of 1929: "Another year and one more record of world-famed achievements by the eminent Miss Nicht-nicht, but don't fear; great things are bound to transpire." On the negative side, the commentaries pile up: "It seems a blasphemy to let time pass by doing nothing." "If I could only earn money" was a constant refrain, especially after the statement that appears on November 12, 1929, regarding the "temperamental stock market." Defining myself at one point as an "antique adolescent," I also mourned—when I was not yet twenty-one—"my lost youth." As for my productivity, "my pen is dry and my mind nearly so." And later, "Personally I don't think I'll ever amount to anything but a lot of talk."

The strain continues in the new decade. "Don't let me waste the rest of my life." "I will walk to the ladder of success, but do I climb?" "There doesn't seem much hope to getting anything." "I don't want to bank too much on fruitless dreams." Reading *Nana* and casting my first vote for FDR—"making the country safer for democracy"—I continued my writing: a story called "Deuces Released," another entitled "The Russian Approach." "Will continue so long as my muse hovers about."

The muse certainly hovered. In 1931, my readings and my intellectual interests intensified. I plunged into the writings of Katherine Mansfield, Somerset Maugham, and especially *Jean Christophe,* the interminable novel by Romain Rolland. I actually read this last in the original French. I had seen it in a multivolume paperback edition at the Stechert Bookstore on 12th Street, and bought it—not as a set, but volume by volume over the months. The text was uplifting, but my feat was more so. I thrilled especially to Galsworthy's *Forsyte Saga*. When he lectured at the Brooklyn Academy of Music, I trekked there during a torrential downpour, listened avidly to his talk about invalid authors who wrote cheerful books, and wrote him a letter of gratitude as soon as I returned home. My reward came a few weeks later, when John Galsworthy wrote to thank Leona Rostenberg and to hope that "you were none the worse for Brooklyn that wet night." Galsworthy inspired not only my praise but my pen, and I soon attempted a family saga of my own, along with a flurry of short stories—"The Rag," "Genius," "Coming Home." All of them were duly dispatched to popular magazines: *Liberty, Collier's, Harper's*—and all duly came home.

Despite the accumulation of rejection slips, the act of creating uplifted me and, at the same time, often during the same weeks and months, the negative was counteracted—blasted away—by the positive. Shortly after Miss Nicht-nicht's self-reproaches, she called herself "such a dumb optimist at times that I can't see clearly and oh the force of daydreaming." Determination speedily empowered the "antique adolescent," who wrote: "I'm no longer in that insane adolescent period." Even more affirmatively I declared: "Everyone wants to accomplish something but I shall, I will and that's final." And a bit later: "I feel something is coming, but I can't get it out, just like a melody unsung." Again: "I feel I have a destiny and yet I shift my temperament from the silliest of daydreams to the loftiest of Olympian heights." "I must accomplish something," I exclaimed. "This magnificent urge that keeps one going."

It did keep me going. I cogitated, "The world of fame calls me and I wonder if it's more alluring than matrimony. . . . Been busy with my German Renaissance paper. It's finished and it's a true masterpiece. Came out first on Kramer's exam—quite a triumph." That triumph called forth larger ambitions. "I feel a desire for being learned, to address large classes of admiring pupils and such."

My two selves—the confident and the lost—came together when I pondered seriously "the question of my future—the dawn of youth finds its horizon bleak and I'm really anxious to do something, get out, accomplish . . ." It would be out of the bleakness, out of the transient failure, that my triumph would eventually be wrested. One day I would say to an interviewer, "I was nothing. Madeleine made my life." But Madeleine by that time was saying to the same interviewer, "I was nothing. Leona made my life."

Both of these comments were true, for having found each other, we were enabled to find ourselves.

MADELEINE

One reason for the despair reflected in some pages of Leona's diary was the realization that most of her women friends were pairing off, marrying, and having children. The diaries record her love of children as well as her relationship with a series of male companions. Although at one point she wrote, "I've decided not to marry young," she was obviously disturbed by the succession of wedding ceremonies she witnessed and the infants to whom she presented rattles or nighties. Her fluctuation from pessimism to optimism fascinated me much more than it troubled me, and by the time I had enrolled for my master's at Columbia, I was beginning to regard myself as an analyst of the multiple personality. I had studied it in a college course on abnormal psychology. Now I felt I was studying it in my friend Leona. And, as a graduate student in English, I was especially inspired to study the phenomenon in literature.

I began with my master's essay on Mary Magdalene, and was especially intrigued by the problem of her identity. There were three Marys who may have been one Mary. In addition to Mary Magdalene, there was Mary the sister of Martha; and there was the sinner of Luke VII. There was a rejoicing Mary and a weeping Mary; there was a Mary who was prostitute and midwife and a Mary who was holy apostle, a virgin and martyr. Surely if all the Marys were inhabitants of one body, my Mary Magdalene was a multiple personality. My conclusions, based on my twenty-page bibliography, were ambivalent: "In the face of . . . differing opinions, it is difficult to arrive at a conclusion. . . . Saint Mary Magdalene . . . may have been three persons . . . her identity and her tomb are sources of debate . . . during the Middle Ages in the West she was believed to be one person."

The theme of multiple personality continued to

engross me. My first published article would be entitled "Hungry Ghosts: Flux of Identity in Contemporary Literature." In it, I transferred my pursuit of dual personality into the twentieth century, tracing contemporary interest in the mutations of self. My sources now were modern rather than medieval—André Gide and Proust, Pirandello and Dostoevsky, Conrad Aiken, Victoria Sackville-West, T. S. Eliot. From their pages I ferreted out their thoughts on multiplicity of the ego, ending my scholarly survey light-heartedly with the remark: "The writer thinks it about time she took the infinity of her selves for an airing."

My article was published in 1935 in the *Sewanee Review.* Many years later, largely as a result of Leona's researches and discoveries, I would pursue another dual life—the double literary life of Louisa May Alcott.

Now, in the early 1930s, when Leona and I were meeting for lunch on the Columbia campus, comparing notes on our studies and readings, making dates for movies or theaters, I was finishing up what would be my first published book—a study less of multiple personality than of the personalities of my friends and the nature of my own self.

Unlike *Mary Magdalene in Medieval Literature* and unlike "Hungry Ghosts," *We Are Taken* is an ambitious first novel, almost entirely autobiographical in nature, that depicts the characters and early life stories of my friends and myself. Leona is not a character in this book, which had been projected before our reunion. But the friends of my adolescence are, and I myself am the lonely observer of their romances and their courtships.

On the framework of "The Farmer in the Dell," I constructed a story that ends with myself—the nineteen-year-old Elinor King—standing alone, like the Cheese in the nursery rhyme. Part I, "Entrance to the Dell," presents a fairly accurate and conscientious recapturing of my childhood. Part II, "In the Dell," reanimates my school friends, Lee, Ann, and Nina. Nina is the special friend with whom I share my adolescent fabrications—my dreamed-up thirty-room house in England, my imaginary grandparents—a forthright Huguenot and an Italian count. With Nina, I act out my romanticism, my belief that all right and all wrong must be judged by nothing but great truth and great beauty. Our relationship is a substitute relationship in which eroticism and romanticism mingle. It is depicted as a substitute, a preparation, a hope, an anticipation of a more passionate heterosexual relationship.

The male partners are introduced in Part III, "Departure from the Dell." There we meet the boys— the poetic Lawrence with the Byronic soul; the gallant Edwin; the humor-loving, fascinating Richard; the Irish Catholic-turned-atheist, Joey. In the end, Elinor's friends—my friends—pair off, leaving Elinor standing alone:

> *Elinor would not be content with such men as these.*
>
> *She would resist their unholy temptation. For there was no doubt about it that the security and peace they offered were tempting. But she would refrain. . . . She was wretched in the thought that the others—her dear friends— had not refrained.*

She says to Nina in the end, "I can only stand still before the rush of time. . . . We're growing up. . . . But I'm still free."

We Are Taken is a very young book by a very young writer. It is dedicated to my mother, whose stalwart figure and warm humanity pervade the story. She is removed from me and my friends by a generation or more, but she emerges as "the only thing that was not new and could still be clung to with surety." *We Are Taken* is also a very revealing book—in a way a counterpart of sorts to Leona's diaries—by a young author in love with love, in love with words, but not in love with the lovers she dated. The men whom Elinor King never married were also the men whom Madeleine Stern never married. As Elinor King stood alone, watching the pairing-off of her friends, so did Madeleine Stern. And in an unwritten sequel to *We Are Taken* Madeleine would find not the lover, not the husband, but the friend of a lifetime.

La Triomphe des Femmes, ou il est montré . . . que le Sexe Feminin, est plus noble & plus parfait que le masculin [The Triumph of Women, in which it is demonstrated . . . that the female sex is nobler and more perfect than the male]. C.M.D. Noel, French, 1700

Condemnation of the role of master assigned to himself by man, and support of woman's superiority to man. Bound in calf.

Acquired by the Folger Shakespeare Library, 1974

Chapter Three

THE MEN WE DID NOT MARRY

MADELEINE

During the 1930s, especially the early thirties, I formed friendships with a succession of young men. All of them were more or less, as they said in those days, "eligible"—that is, marriageable. Though they had prospects, none had money. But, then, who did in the Depression years? Half of them had non-German, more specifically, Russian ancestry. But who else had migrated in greater droves to the States? All were Jewish. Jews then were thrown together and seldom mingled socially with non-Jews. Each young man had something to recommend him for possible matrimony, and in the 1930s matrimony was the dream of most young women. However talented or sophisticated they might be, marriage was their expected destiny.

91

I could not help sharing some of that attitude. When I saw my friends walk down the aisle with bouquets of orange blossoms, I envisioned myself in their place. But I was never fully convinced that marriage was to be my be-all and my end-all. Certainly my mother never tried to sway me in that direction, though she doubtless silently appraised my dates as possible mates.

During some of those years I was earning money as a teacher of English, first in Theodore Roosevelt High School in the Bronx, and later in Long Island City High School in Queens. I could be independent of a man's support. But I longed to give up teaching for a career as a writer. When I tried to picture my future, I saw myself as a writer, perhaps married, perhaps not. I dreamed of throwing off the fetters of teaching high school English far more than I longed to throw off any fetters of living at home with my mother. Being a writer, a researcher, an intellectual explorer was the important thing. Being married was less important.

The young men who crossed my path did nothing to change my attitude. Being with them might be a broadening experience, but it was an experience, I discovered, that I would rather discuss with Leona than actually live.

The first young man I dated was, as I realize now, probably the most "eligible." He came from a proper upper-middle-class Jewish family, and he had been schooled in the niceties of social behavior. He looked pleasant, and he was pleasant. Unfortunately, he was not very dynamic. We were introduced to each other—such introductions were often fairly formal— by my mother's cousin, who had developed quite a reputation for match-making or at least for trying to match-make. I was only in my late teens and had not had any experience to speak of in being with boys. The schools I attended were all-girl institutions.

For our first date, my first boyfriend, who bore my brother's name, Leonard, invited me to a tea dance. My dancing was not great, despite my early tutoring at dancing school, nor was his, but we managed to get through a few rounds fairly decently, combining polite conversation with more or less awkward steps.

He did "ask me out" again, and while nothing

exciting ever occurred, I was learning how to let a boy hold my coat or pull out my chair, and to accept delicate politesse with a modicum of ease. We never kissed, much less petted.

Through his practice with me, Leonard Benjamin was probably polishing his own social graces. He introduced me to his parents, and he presented me with a pin—the symbol of a closer relationship in a ceremony known as "pinning a girl." But such a relationship somehow never developed. The last time we saw each other was at the football game between Syracuse and Columbia, to which he invited me for Thanksgiving Day. I knew as much about football as I knew about men. I might hide my ignorance about the latter, but I could not hide it about the former. I shouted when the wrong side won; often I could not distinguish a win from a loss; by the end of the game I was not only hoarse but dismayed and, worse still, bored. Poor Leonard Benjamin tried to make the best of a bad bargain, and I am sure that eventually he made someone a fine husband. As for me, I learned as little about sex as I did about football, and I kept his pin— the wrong thing to do.

I learned more about romance and glamour from my next major male companion. Albert Trepuk was the perfect teacher, the perfect conveyor of that tenuous, unsubstantial feeling that sometimes defines a relationship. My relationship with Albert was like that—glamorous but not substantial. It was another of my mother's cousins who brought us together. He had been a close friend of Albert's father, who served as a diplomat from Belgium in the consulate of St. Thomas, Virgin Islands. Albert was several years my senior, but enormously attractive and filled with what was to me the occultism of another world. He was an incomparable spinner of tales of the voodoo he had heard in the West Indies and now repeated for my benefit. He thrilled me with magical incantations and mystic rites. As a matter of fact, he talked more than he listened, and that came to bother me. It was not till much later that I learned the duplicity of my magician from St. Thomas. While he was escorting me to the theater or regaling me with weird and ghostly stories, he was also conducting a tempestuous affair with "an older woman" who lived conveniently near me. The last time I had a date with Albert was the night my father died. When I returned home on September 24, 1930, I had begun telling my parents about my evening when my father, who had already had a succession of minor strokes, had a major one and died in moments. Although my mother must have known he was dead, I was not sure, never having seen death before. In the context in which it happened—while I was telling my insignificant story of an evening with a young man—it seemed impossible. My father, whose straightforwardness and certainty characterized his life, had died while I was repeating the eerie episodes of Albert's ghostly tales. My association of Albert with enticing magic took on a more ominous and sober tinge—a taint. I associated him now less with romance than with death. My flirtation with Albert and with voodoo was over.

The man who followed in Albert's wake was far more of this world than of a ghostly one. I met Mortie Braus at the wedding of my close friends Shirley Phillips and Alvin Cowan. I was maid of honor; Mortie was an usher. It was an elaborate ceremony, with about two hundred guests, so grand indeed that Mortie and I were glad to pair off together. He talked mostly of his work as a lawyer, which was not very satisfying for him. As a lawyer he had strong views about the Lindbergh baby kidnapping and the imprisonment of Al Capone. As a fashionable young man, he warmly admired my finery—my maid of honor's costume, an orange taffeta evening dress. He took me home and made another date. As far as I was concerned, there was only one thing wrong with Mortie Braus. Despite his elegant tux, despite his intelligent conversation, Mortie Braus was overweight. My passions were not aroused.

His avoirdupois notwithstanding, we formed a steady friendship, in the course of which I learned much about sophisticated New York life. Prohibition was still with us in 1932, as it had been for all the years I was growing up. As a result, and although my father had once been in the liquor business, I knew absolutely nothing about spiritous beverages. None ever crossed the lips of any diners at our table, and though we enjoyed many happy hours at home, we had no "happy hour." Prohibition had enlarged the American vernacular with two much-used words: "bootlegging" and "speakeasy." If Al Capone's exploits taught me about the former, Mortie Braus introduced me to the latter.

It was quite an experience. We passed through the door of a small building after my escort whispered a mysterious secret code through the peephole. We entered what appeared to be an ordinary restaurant, with chairs and tables, most of them meant for two. When we were seated a waiter appeared and Mortie promptly gave his order: "A Tom Collins for me." Then he looked at me, questioning, eyebrows raised. I hesitated. I had no idea what to order. Only one course seemed open to me. "I'll have one too." Mortie relaxed and seemed pleased. I was curious. What would I get? What had I done?

It was my first and my last Tom Collins, since gin would never be a favorite with me. Prohibition itself would not last much longer, and with its end would come the end of the speakeasy. But in 1932 Prohibition was an unfortunate, a disastrous American institution. The speakeasy was America's response, contrived to counteract a puerile form of censorship. Thanks to Mortie Braus, I saw it in action.

Another American institution to which Mortie

introduced me was the music of Guy Lombardo. We danced to it at the Hotel Roosevelt, both of us dressed to the nines. As we danced, we discussed the play we had seen together. Mortie was a frequent escort when I reviewed performances for the Barnard paper. It was all very pleasant and, I thought, highly sophisticated. We danced until the band leader played "Good night sweetheart—good night till tomorrow."

In that tomorrow, however, Mortie played no part. He gave up the law, moved to California, and wrote or doctored scripts for Hollywood. After *We Are Taken* was published, he wrote to me to express his semiprofessional view, which seemed less helpful than puzzling:

> *I found it almost as attention compelling as* The Postman Always Rings Twice. . . . *The uncanny mastery of technique and word blending just stunned me, not to mention the virtuosic treatment of a most fragile theme. . . .*
>
> *Where you fail is in the texture of your tapestry. I, for one, regret the lack of coloration and pigmentation. Simple chiarascuro*

is not enough to win a lasting place in the fic-
tion firmament. In other words you haven't
orchestrated your melody. It remains at most
a string quartet.

Indeed. And one could say the same for my relationship with Mortie Braus.

If Mortie was too stout for my taste, the physical
appearance of the next incumbent—Bernie Klauber—
was so unmarked that I have truly forgotten what he
looked like. Bernie was, as far as his relationship with
me was concerned, an unembodied intellect.

There were no speakeasy tête-à-têtes with
Bernard Klauber, M.D. By the time we met, the
speakeasy was a phenomenon of the past. There was
no dancing to Guy Lombardo or to any other band
leader. There was a great deal of talking, of which
most was soliloquizing. Every once in a while Bernie
would punctuate his monologues by whipping out a
pad and recording some profound bon mot I had
managed to interject in what was always a one-sided
conversation.

I had met Bernie through a high school friend—

the Nina of *We Are Taken,* who by the mid-thirties was married to a physician. Bernie had recently achieved his M.D. degree, and around the same time, for reasons unknown to me, changed his name from Goldberg to Klauber. To say that he *practiced* in the Bronx was a euphemism. His practice, as far as I could make out, was nonexistent. He devoted hours to talk and even more hours to letter-writing. He wrote until he had no more paper. When I discussed him and his turgid, ponderous epistles with Leona, as I was coming to do more and more, her succinct and very apt comment was, "He can't have too many patients."

Bernie's talk led to his letters, and his letters were fuel for his talk. My current interest in tracing techniques of proletarian literature in America for the *Sewanee Review* led him to comment on "the fashionable mania of the literati that all serious modern literature is proletarian. If the aspiring young dramatist writes a play about coal mines or Sacco and Vanzetti, he is keeping the faith." The fascism that was beginning to erupt overseas caused him to muse, "What gave rise to fascism if not the deep nationalist instincts in the people?" Communism was a staple of his conversation. He anatomized Kant and Bergson. As he himself said, during our sessions together he heaved "intellectual snowballs" at me "from the moment we meet to the moment we part."

Although he wrote, "I'd like to see your eyes blaze. I'd like to see you aflame. I'd like you to tell me what you really think of me," he never set me on fire nor did he give me much opportunity to tell him what I really thought of him.

He was free and easy, however, with his thoughts about me and our relationship. At one point he wrote, "Your letters are strangely in contrast with the way you talk to me when I am with you. With a pen in your hand, you are a different girl. Your dry, pointed humor is discarded for dreamy ponderings and creamy linguistics." As for the nature of our relationship, he observed with accuracy:

> *For you to know that the sexual aura of man-woman relationship is foreign to our friendship . . . is fine and true. . . . I like you in a bigger way than before because you seem to*

*know your own feelings as well as I know
mine. Your answer to my assertion that you
are not poetic or meditative with me is precisely the answer that I would make if you re-
proached me for not being amorous and
glamorous with you. . . . The word "pla-
tonic," needn't be sarcastically dragged in
to excuse the lack of sex.*

During his first year in practice, Bernie experienced what he described as "horrible nerve-wracking
calm." Leona was right. No patients flocked to his
Bronx door. And so he began to write a play about the
modern physician and the plight of the "passionately
idealistic medical student" who is "plunged into the
mess of private practice." His protagonist was Jewish,
without funds, caught up in "a cold-blooded business" and forced to take himself too seriously "in order to hoax the public into belief of his competency."
Bernie's hero was Bernie, whose path momentarily
crossed that of Madeleine–Alice in Wonderland.

His place was soon taken by another young
physician, who happened to be Leona's older brother.

Dr. Adolph Rostenberg, Jr., seemed on the surface to be the most eligible of my young men. He came from the same German-Jewish background as I did and was some six years my elder. As far as his profession was concerned, he had boldly begun his medical career as a specialist in his father's field, dermatology. He was the senior doctor's junior associate, and although the patients who came to the door came for Senior and not Junior, Junior's prospects seemed rosy enough. Although not prepossessing in appearance—he was on the short side—Adolph had a mass of attractive carrot-red hair, which earned him the nickname of Rusty. Rusty had a penetrating and catholic mind. He was always in pursuit of some demanding hobby, from the mathematics of infinity to botany and horticulture, from stamp-collecting and card-playing to word games and fishing. He had so many hobbies that I, trying to keep up with him, earned the epithet of "whim-caterer" from my friends. Adolph, in short, was interesting. Any uncertainty about his eligibility was soon dispelled, for Adolph was extremely eager to be married.

During the period of what might be called his

courtship, it began to dawn on me that although Adolph was determined to be married, he was not at all determined to be married to me. For me, the best part of the whole affair was that he was Leona's brother. That relationship endeared him to me far more than any of his own attributes. Leona, who could not forget her role as Adolph's scorned "kid sister," questioned his seriousness. At the same time, she hoped for a closer relationship between her friend and her brother, believing it would bring her even closer to me.

However, I was gradually learning that his major attribute—the one that overshadowed all the others—was his concept of woman. Adolph was no egalitarian. Woman, he actually believed, was made to serve man. Woman was—or should be—man's inferior. In the mid-1930s the expression "macho male" was not yet popular. But Dr. Adolph Rostenberg, Jr., prefigured it. I recall his telling me once that a man owns a woman, especially in marriage.

I still have four of Adolph's letters to me, all undated but written around 1935, which more or less define our relationship. All are filled with his love of words, expletives, alliteration, of puzzles and games and mental gymnastics. His affection for me is curiously shrouded in the sweep of adjectives he uses to admonish me for going away and leaving him alone over one weekend. I was, he wrote, "careless + thoughtless + exhibitionist + inconsiderate + . . . uneconomical + social climbing + lacking in devotion," all of which added up to "unmitigated louse." "In fact," he concluded, "I think I have been euphemistic. I do hope you will mend your ways and wend your footsteps to an early return to the city in order that I might personally admonish you." His coda clearly reflects the condescension of the macho male: "Incidentally, admonishing wayward girls is something at which I am especially adept—you would be surprised to see how tractable they become after a judicious selection of the proper admonishment." His final reference to his letter as a "farrago" is accompanied by the advice to this teacher of English—"look that one up."

The right background, the right age, the right profession, the brilliant mind—all these together could not compensate for such an attitude. Adolph

106

soon married a far more "tractable" bride, and I began dating another marital candidate.

I had heard something of Bill Steckler's glories from a neighbor in our apartment house, but I did not meet him until the year 1935 was turning into the year 1936. It was a hilarious New Year's Eve party in Dover, New Jersey, that Leona, her friend Lucy, and I attended after ferrying across the Hudson and hitchhiking in Jersey. With those present, including my friend Helen, her Raymond, and the celebrated and good-looking Bill Steckler, we went ice skating and screamed much of the night away as loud talk was topped by louder laughter. I don't recall much of Bill Steckler from that evening, except that with much fanfare he placed upon a bed a copy of a recent popular novel entitled *It Can't Happen Here*.

As a matter of fact, it did not happen there, and I did not give much thought to Bill Steckler until he called to make a date. Bill was an attractive young man with a creative mind. A lawyer in the Justice Department, specifically the Bureau of Immigration, he devoted much of his leisure to music. Bill was a good enough violinist, and I was his audience when he performed in solo or with his amateur string quartet. Despite his artistic inclinations, there was a strong streak of the vulgar in Bill, and he did not hesitate to bark out four-letter words when he disapproved of something. But Bill attracted me, and during one summer, after a tedious period of teaching English in high school, I suggested to my mother that we spend a few weeks in the Adirondacks, where Bill was vacationing with his older sister and her husband. My mother was acquiescent if not enthusiastic. Bill was enthusiastic. He wrote to me: "It really isn't so bad, this best of possible worlds. It may very well be that the Adirondacks will charm you as they have me. This is truly thrilling country. You will find here an infinite number of things to absorb your restless mind. . . . We will have fun, you can be sure."

We did have fun. We climbed mountains, we talked, we enjoyed each other's company. However, it was made perfectly clear to me that Bill's family was disinclined to see their bright young star trapped so early in the confines of matrimony. And, unlike Adolph, Bill had not yet set his sights on a closer union. In fact, he feared the permanence it entailed. Our relationship may have struck fire, but it could not endure. In a letter to me, he wrote, "My impression of the night and morning just gone are that the wind, a girl and a book seem exceeding good, that sleep did not come and yet I am rested. A pretty non sequitur, what?" He did not specify the direction of the wind, the identity of the girl, or the title of the book. And after these many years, I cannot remember.

And so the interaction of half a dozen young men in my life led to one conclusion. My six men were six reasons I would never marry. After my varied experiences, I was still a single woman in a man's world.

LEONA

There were always boys and young men in the house. My brother, three and a half years my senior, brought home friends from school and the neighborhood. Among the latter were his associates from an estimable society, the Concourse Bicycle Club. It seems their purpose was not to ride at high speed along the

Grand Concourse, but, rather, to gather at his home to smash Ping-Pong balls, exchange jokes, make a racket, and throw ice cream bricks at one another. Occasionally one of the bricks found the wrong target and hit the kid sister. As it happened, she didn't mind. One of the boys—a handsome all-American teenager—caught her immature fancy. More important, though the ways of the world eluded her, she was becoming familiar with the ways of young boys.

Despite my early association with American boys, the male companions of my youth had foreign backgrounds. Unlike Madeleine's boyfriends, mine were all German-born. Karl Flanter had never been a member of the Concourse Bicycle Club. His origins were utterly remote. Like my father, he hailed from Königsberg, in East Prussia. Trained in his father's haberdashery, he disliked the ways of his native Germany and, in the spring of 1929, sought a new future in the New World. One of the assets he carried with him was a letter of introduction to my father, who had been a casual acquaintance of the elder Flanter. The Rostenbergs gave the newcomer a cordial greeting. And I, confronting this amiable and handsome foreigner, welcomed him to America. For some five years, from the time I was twenty, Karl Flanter was an intermittent presence in my life and in my heart.

Like most young immigrants at the time, Karl had come to America to improve himself, to make money, to brighten his uncertain future. His qualifications for success were not noteworthy. Karl was no intellectual; he was far from overeducated; in fact he had not even completed the courses at the Königsberg Gymnasium. But Karl was—especially to a twenty-year-old girl in search of romance—highly desirable. He was handsome, although his delicate features gave him a slightly effeminate appearance. There was nothing of male chauvinism about this tall, neatly dressed foreigner. He had come to our door in search of a better life. I would invest him with my dreams in my search for love.

My first diary entry about him was penned on July 9, 1929: "Karl came up. Sometimes I think I'm in love with him. I think I really want him to kiss me. He was so adorable. I might be Mrs. Flanter, but then so much has to be considered. Someday my mind shall be settled." That day was still far off. Less than a week later I had begun seesawing about this gallant: "He . . . just takes everything as a matter of course. I became very angry and didn't talk to him. The fuss the folks made over him. I'm tired of the whole thing."

In spite of his physical attraction, I was beginning to look beneath the surface, resenting not only my parents' so obvious—perhaps pretended—enthusiasm, but Karl's own inadequacies. The conflict created an ambivalence in my emotions that lasted for at least four years, through other entanglements. While I was self-searching, I was also love-searching, and my enchantment wavered with my disenchantment.

My conflicting emotions were recorded in my diary. And, between the lines, were reflected my perplexity, my total lack of understanding about this young man's inner nature and his attitude toward me. He seemed often to be more attracted to my mother than to me. Of course, she, who had been a Southern belle, still had a way with men and knew how to put them at ease. At times I suspected that Karl was seeking not a lovesick young woman but a surrogate mother. There was a mystery about him that I would never fathom. One of the mysteries connected with

Karl was that he kept returning to me. Week after week, month after month, and year after year, he came to visit or escort me to a movie or a play or a concert—once even to a burlesque show. If he cared for me, however, he scarcely showed it. It was a static companionship that got nowhere, but, susceptible as I was in my early twenties, it left me in turmoil.

My diary reflects the ups and downs of our relationship, my bewildered struggle to understand his feelings for me, and my own vacillating reactions. On February 23, 1930, months after he had first appeared, I pontificated: "Karl likes me no doubt as a clever kid, but he doesn't love me. I think if I were of lower moral appeal, he'd take more liberties." By early November I felt sure of my love for him: "Karl called up. Either I'm a romantic fool or a sentimental donkey, but I know this—if he ever asked me to marry him, I wouldn't hesitate. He was his old sweet self this evening, sympathetic, etc. Seeing him Sunday night. Doubt whether he knows how much I care for him." On November 9, "Met Karl at the Commodore. I got a thrill when he came in. He looked so lovely. . . . I want to love him, but I suppose it's just not up to that point as yet." Toward the end of the month the emotional climate had chilled: "Karl is coming Thursday, going to another dinner in the eve. I'm afraid it's rather over on his part. I'll get off when I know that I'm not wanted. I hate *dead leaves*." But after a happy New Year's Eve with Karl, I rose to the summit of joy: "I have never ended a year with such supreme feelings for anyone, that darling boy. Oh Lord, it was glorious! Karl, how easily I could eternally remain with you, and I think you know."

Two months later, in February 1931, my emotional seesaw was down on the ground: "Upon waking this A.M. I discovered one important factor. I'm all over Karl. It isn't coz he doesn't come anymore, but I don't get a peculiar heart throb when I think of him. Well, it was nice." Nonetheless, it took only another few weeks for the return of heart throbs: "Met Karl. Went to Roxy's. Got home at 2 A.M. I can't help it, but I do like him tremendously. There's a surge and a definite sexual attraction, tho I can never really now imagine him as my husband. I told him I was engaged. The result—boy, what consternation." In August when Karl came up, "He was adorable. We're awfully good friends & he feels so at home here. It's all very comforting." Karl was still "coming up" in October. He was still "adorable." But "Sometimes I wonder how it would be . . . if we were married. You can't get under his skin."

By December I was still suffering the "inner turmoil. Karl is up to his old tricks again. Oh let's call the thing over rather than this foolish clinging hope. Of course I like him, but will that settle anything." A week later, when Karl arrived, "we talked the entire nite. . . . I told him I can't really understand him, try as I will." There is no doubt that Karl was always a mystery.

By September 1932 I had enrolled for graduate study at Columbia, and Karl, with my father's help, had found employment in a glove factory in the appropriate location of Gloversville, New York. Though he came back and forth with some degree of frequency, our dates were casual. I still could not "get under his skin." As I confided to my diary: "I don't want to feel indifferent, but he's multi-sided, & one minute I love his profile—the next second I'm bored with his bidding." At the end of the month I reported the finale in my journal: "The affair of Karl Flanter Esq. & LR, potential M.A., is all over & asunder."

I never did get under Karl's skin, though I continued to ponder his peculiarities. Years later I would wonder if perhaps he was a homosexual and, like many homosexuals, happy in the company of an older woman. Certainly his pleasure in my mother's company suggested something of this nature. Many years later I did learn, from a distant relative, that Karl had finally married an older woman, a widow with two children. I cannot forget, though, that in his youth he set me on fire, and that is how I must remember him.

If the ardor of Karl Flanter was invisible at times, the enthusiasm of François Ritter for his American student was ever present. I had come to Strasbourg in 1936 to research my doctoral dissertation on the influence of the early Strasbourg printers on the spread of humanism and the Reformation. The topic had not found favor with my Columbia University mentor, Lynn Thorndike, who regarded the printers as mere hacks, but—young and brash and sure of myself—I persisted. In Strasbourg I found not only a wealth of supportive source material, but a scholar who shared my view and endorsed my premise. His name was François Ritter, but it had not always been so. He was born Franz Ritter, and in 1914 he had served as a private in the German army. His native Strasbourg had long been a football between France and Germany, and after World War I, when France was in the ascendancy, Franz became François. An excellent scholar, now in his early fifties, he was, by the time I met him, chief of the Rare Books Department in the Bibliothèque Universitaire et Publique. Tall and blue-eyed, he was pleasing in appearance for what I then regarded as an "elderly" man.

My first visits to the library and my first encounters with Monsieur Ritter are recorded in my diary: " . . . For every book you take out they charge 1 fr 50—oh for Columbian democracy. . . . But I cheat them; I borrow the books from Ritter, who has installed practically the whole library in his office. . . . he's been swell & I'm popping in & out of his office— discussing things in German with great authority." Though Franz had become François, we usually spoke only German to each other, as did most of the citizens of this Alsatian city. It was not long before Ritter's eagerness to help me with my research was complemented with another kind of ardor. Both the Teutonic nature of Strasbourg and the amatory nature of my librarian would become more and more pronounced as the autumn months of 1936 rolled on.

The German affiliations of this officially French city of Strasbourg were reflected in my diary from the beginning of my residence there. When I "went out to the Rhine" I was at first "sorry I didn't have my passport; it may have been a lark to cross into Germany, but when I stood on the Pont à Kehl & saw those Nazi standards, something hit me so very hard that I winced & drew back. I wanted to fight & spit—I did spit & how I hated what lay on the other side of that sluggish stream." I did not hate what lay on "my" side of the Rhine. Walking in my trench coat past newspaper kiosks and *drogueries,* past wagons and harness-makers' shops, past donkeys wearing earcaps and past the vaulting glass of the great Cathedral, I reveled in the city, feeling the centuries of history past, and I wrote in my diary: "If Madeleine were here, this would be a very perfect life."

"Bookends," London, 1937

Madeleine's great-grandfather,
Isaac Rauh,
and great-grandmother,
Magdalena Mack Rauh,
after whom she was named,
ca. 1850

Leona's mother, Louisa Dreyfus, at 24, painted in Berlin, ca. 1894

Three photos by Abbey Lustgarten from oil paintings

Engagement pictures of Roland Stern and
Lillie Mack, Thanksgiving 1901

Leona's future parents, Louisa Dreyfus and Adolph Rostenberg, in 1902

Leona at nine years

Madeleine at nine months

Madeleine with her big brother, Leonard Mack Stern, ca. 1914

Leona versus her big brother, Adolph Rostenberg, Jr., ca. 1912

Bon voyage to Leona from her
mother, SS *California*, 1937

Mother Lillie and baby
Madeleine, Summer 1913

The trio—Madeleine, Lillie,
Leona—in Maine, 1938

Leona at
Sunnybank, Maine,
1941

Madeleine at the
Menin gate, Ypres,
1937

Adolph Rostenberg, Jr., ca. 1935

Leona with François Ritter, her romantic librarian of 1936

At the first New York Antiquarian Book Fair, 1960

At Victoria Peak,
Hong Kong, 1973

Our Japanese
business card,
1973

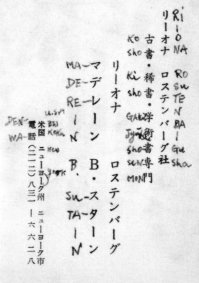

Madeleine and Leona, Chicago, 1974

At our New York Book Fair booth ca. 1980
with bookseller Paulette Rose

"Bookends" at work in East Hampton, 1996

Leona on the
Bay Beach,
East Hampton,
1998

Indulgent Chimpie

Louisa May

Bettina

Laurie with Leona,
Mary Bertschmann,
and Madeleine

"Bookends" at home, 2001

At first, librarian Ritter was simply part of that colorful and fascinating background. He "allows me many liberties" in the library, expedites my research and is "a love." "Ritter," as my diary testifies, "can't do enough. Have my morning chat with darling François & today we conversed in French about nothing in particular."

Ritter was always there in the background of my studies, and his generous, helpful, caring attentions came to be fused with my growing love of books. He seemed to be part of them when I "fondled . . . these works which Erasmus had played with, these editions printed at Paris & Venice at Forli & Augsburg at Rome & Cologne in . . . Anno Domini 1509." But as my love of books increased, so too did François' love of me, until it became what I described as "a real problem." Ritter was not only a married man but— impossible even to contemplate—a grandfather, although admittedly a young one. "I think this is serious," I confided to my diary. "There's little doubt left that dear sweet Ritter's falling in love with me. God knows what I'm going to do about it. He's lovable but he has a grandchild . . . & a religious wife,

Thérèse . . . I like him becoz he helps me & becoz we have nice chats. He looks at me very mournfully & certainly holds my hand a great deal for a librarian. He insists that I stay longer & come back. . . . Poor old thing. . . . Of course François is a young grandpa."

The young grandpa's attentions were now beginning to interfere with rather than expedite my research. As I complained to my diary, "I certainly am having my hands full with my lover—He sighs & groans; holds my hand the entire time I'm in his office—get nothing done; kisses my hand, & can hardly control himself from grabbing me—Today he said he can't stand it any longer—I had better go back to America; he can't work—he can't think—he asked me whether I didn't like him just a little bit & the way he looks at me—we went into the stacks & then I realized my time was nearly up—He stood with his arms opened wide & said aber jetzt [but now] . . . & I said—aber nein [but no]—Ich bin eine geschäftsfrau [I am a business woman]—he rushed ahead madly & slumped into his chair—I don't know what to do. He's very valuable for my work—the old fox—& he sits & moans & looks at me; now he tells me he's coming here [to the pension]—I'll kick him out—This is M. F. Ritter Legionnaire d'honneur— . . . —he's a darling but oh my—I didn't count this in my printing business."

Swiftly now the scenario of François' one-sided love affair developed. Its stages were recorded in my journal as my Alsatian weeks passed by: "François' ardor hasn't cooled at all—he sits with his hand on his brow & his eyes tear as he looks upon his American filly—consequently I don't get any material from him—some mess—Today he said he couldn't wait until I came—how he wants me if he only weren't married . . . & he began to stroke my leg—I became annoyed & slapped him—he apologized & said the whole thing is impossible—ach—er liebt mich so, so viel [he loves me so, so much]—it's really ridiculous—the old gink." Time passed but "My lover is still sufficiently active to really become a nuisance. He followed me to the fair; today visited me in my room, made passionate love & I had to use force. . . . I told him the whole thing is ridiculous;—he's become a problem—& I can't have it—The dear grandpapa retorted he's like Goethe—I'm the only joy in his life. The only thing lovely & dear—'Süss and lieb'—I told him he wasn't Goethe & that I'm not a Romantiker. . . . I don't mind his passion so much, but it's the beer fumes exuding." Those beer fumes "exuding from his amorous mouth" did indeed exacerbate the situation. As I exploded in my diary, "His amours antics included so much Adelshofer . . . that I was almost asphyxiated." Coupled with all this was my lover's insistence upon reading my journal, and so "I have to lock you away" because "I couldn't break his heart any more than I have" and "I told him that he can't come here anymore. . . . This dear grandpa playing with a kitten . . . an old cat."

Despite all that, there was ambivalence in my reactions to François' advances. I might shun his beer fumes, but I could not shun him. Indeed, at one point I wrote: "I don't know, but I'm getting to the point where I could kiss François when he walks toward me with outstretched arms as I enter his office & looks at me with such great love. . . . I find myself going to his office much more frequently than before & not for work—Dear Dear Man . . . François gallant & good

& honest." And again, toward the end of my allotted time: "He's been very sweet & I am really frightened about the dramatics of his farewell. He tells me he's writing love sonnets for my departure." I left Strasbourg in November: "Today I said goodbye to Ritter—realized this eve how deeply he loves me & how truly hard it is for him. . . . The goodbye was long & he was miserable. . . . He gave me a book of love sonnets which he wrote."

I realized at that point, as I realize now, that my relations with François Ritter were interwoven with my love of books and my love of human history. My Strasbourg diary records: "I could write wonders of this life—the special greatness of gleaning into the past & now when I retrospect I feel it & I know it & I'm proud. . . . perhaps by dint of hard labor that century of learning . . . has slowly become part of me & the activity & erudition of 1510 is with me—I don't falter any longer . . . I feel akin to it & my work is my star—I'm glad that I own part of the past, because I can break into the future more securely & more justly—I'm glad of my work—it's there."

Not from books alone but from the scholars I

had met, notable among them my lover François Ritter, "I have gained a love for great books—that is the
art of printing—good printing. I think it will be my
consuming interest—the feel of magnificent bindings;
a beautifully executed edition—an exquisite type—
16c woodcuts & the slow, methodical, but accurate
& careful scholarly approach to any task & above all
the printers of the past. . . . The stamp of my future. I
know my specialty & I want to pursue it & I am will-
ing to work hard becoz I love it."

Strasbourg had given me my future. François
Ritter was part of Strasbourg and would always remain part of my past. After my departure I wrote in
my diary: "François has been lovable, kind, & pa-
tient . . . I don't love him. I never shall, but . . . I will
always know that a man who loves me lives on the
other side of the sea."

The Nazi encroachments that roused my fury in
Strasbourg—the swastikas that waved across the
Rhine—sent me my third suitor. Like Karl, Fritz Levy
was born in Germany, and had studied medicine
there. Unlike Karl, Fritz had left his native land not
out of choice but out of necessity. He might have a

medical degree, but during the Hitler regime there was no way he could develop a medical practice there. Karl was an émigré. Fritz was a refugee. His fortune consisted of forty dollars when he arrived at the golden door. Fritz needed a home and security.

My father's closest friend in Germany had been Robert Levy, Fritz's father. When German Jews were threatened with extinction, nothing was more natural than for Dr. Adolph Rostenberg to sign an affidavit welcoming Dr. Fritz Levy to his adopted country and to his home.

In March of 1938, as the Nazis took Austria, Fritz became part of our household. I waxed enthusiastic in a brief diary entry: "Fritz is with us, a sweet, brave fellow who has nothing but bonhomie & good spirits—Austria is now a part of Germany & Sieg Hitler." Still struggling with my doctoral dissertation, I looked with favor on this young man, with sallow complexion and black hair, who sat at our table, offering polite remarks in German or halting English. For a while I could identify with him. I knew that he was struggling in his way as I was struggling in mine. I had known Fritz as a child when my parents had taken me with them on a trip abroad. I remember a weekend at a seaside resort near Königsberg, Krantz, on the Baltic Sea, where Fritz, dressed in a sailor suit, played in the sand with me. Since then I had not seen him. Now he reappeared, obviously trying to please, but a stranger in a strange land.

The Americanization of Fritz Levy was a long, slow process. Sometimes I thought it would never be achieved. Fritz spent a great deal of time writing letters home—in German; talking to my father—in German; reminiscing with our housekeeper, Babette—in German. Not even his appetite seemed capable of adopting American taste. Occasionally I treated him to lunch at Schrafft's, sometimes with Madeleine. Madeleine and I would sit savoring, devouring, the chocolate fudge sundaes the restaurant was renowned for. After one taste, Fritz would grimace. He had never seen a sweet potato. When I urged one on him, the result was the same—Fritz could not become accustomed to *Amerikanischer Geschmack*. I must confess that I relished discussing him with Madeleine far more than I relished experiencing him alone.

He was, of course, studying for his medical

boards during this period, and for this he had to practice his English. Around the same time he suffered a tragedy when word came that his father—my father's boyhood friend, now a victim of Nazi persecution— had committed suicide. Just a week before, my father had sent him an affidavit to enter the United States. It arrived too late. Fritz seemed to interpret the devastating event as a sign: this country was dilatory in accepting imperiled German Jews.

All this did nothing to encourage the Americanization of Fritz Levy. As the months passed, he no longer seemed the "sweet, brave fellow" I had seen in him at first. Now, in November, I wrote in my diary: "I'm annoyed—I shouldn't write—it's the German in Fritz—the patronizing—I can't stand it." Male chauvinism was difficult to stand in any country, in any language, but in German it seemed particularly distasteful. Added to that was my suspicion that my parents, however subtly, were doing everything in their power to aid and abet a closer union between their daughter and this German refugee they had brought to the States. They gave us concert tickets, because they knew that Fritz was an amateur violinist; they offered us theater tickets; they took advantage of every opportunity to throw us together. Coupled with Fritz's German macho maleness, it made for a situation that I soon found intolerable.

This reaction did not induce me to encourage Fritz's advances. There is no doubt that he did make advances whenever he could, and there is less doubt that if I did not repulse them, I certainly did not encourage them. It was not merely Fritz's nature that swayed me—it was the whole situation in which I was unwillingly involved. I had begun to sense in Fritz a desire to marry, not me, but my father's practice. My parents simply wanted me to marry. I felt that I was being used as a sacrificial offering to satisfy both. However realistic or unrealistic my feeling, I resented it.

Our relationship came to a climactic close after the opening of the New York World's Fair in Flushing, Queens, on April 30, 1939. The fair that styled itself "The World of Tomorrow" was doomed from the start. Its official theme, Progress and Peace, was illusory, a dream conjured up on the very brink of war. Its symbols, the crystal ball Perisphere and the golden Trylon, invited hopeful crowds to parade the fair grounds, to visit the Soviet pavilion, with its statue of laborer and red star, the French, the Belgian, the Italian pavilions. The German pavilion was conspicuous by its absence. Britain and France would declare war on Germany in early September. Most Americans had begun to shun Germany and German things by the time of the fair's opening. Certainly my German-born father had stopped speaking his native language, and German Jews in particular had begun to hate and fear anything that reminded them of the country. With the opening of hostilities in Europe, the fair that had promised the World of Tomorrow lost its lure, and on the first of November it closed its gates.

During the few months that it continued, Madeleine and I visited the fair several times, viewing the exciting General Motors exhibit of future technology, dining at the French pavilion, joining the crowds of still exuberant sightseers on the fair grounds. It was on one of those occasions that we also saw a sight that changed the course of my personal life. Close to the entrance, we encountered an unexpected fair visitor—a familiar figure with sallow complexion and pitchblack hair—the same figure that appeared morning, noon, and night at our family dinner table. This time his arms were not on a table but were encircling the waist of a young woman. My male chauvinist friend had been enjoying a secret romance all the time he was partaking of our hospitality and soliciting my affection.

The discovery marked the virtual end of any relationship between Fritz and myself. Fritz's Americanization would be accomplished not by me but by his service, as F. Robert Levy, in the armed forces of the United States. I would soon become apprenticed to a rare book dealer. Our ways would part and, like Madeleine, I would resume life as a single woman in a man's world.

Das Mutterrecht [The Authority of Motherhood], Johann Jacob Bachofen, German, 1897

Landmark study of motherhood investigating the matriarchal role in society. With seven lithographic plates and two folding plates, bound in original printed wrappers.

Acquired by a private collector, 1992

Chapter Four
MOTHERS

MADELEINE

Life with my father was, alas, relatively short. He died when I was only eighteen. I had my mother far longer, till I was forty-six.

For all those years—during my childhood, my youth, my maturity—she was there, the one certainty in an uncertain world—sustenance, stability, affirmation. By no means did she always agree with me or I with her. She was her own person. But she respected my right to disagree. She helped me become *my* own person. In all my major decisions, in all the watershed events I experienced, she played a role. She was part of me, and she lives in me still.

She was *there*—always. When as a child I came home from school, she was physically there. She must have had dates with friends, gone shopping downtown, played bridge somewhere, but my memory is that at three o'clock she was home, waiting for me, welcoming me. As I grew older, our tie was an intellectual one. She was the listener, the participant, the companion, who shared my interests. Throughout there was an emotional cord that pulled us together. Physically, intellectually, emotionally, we were bound together.

I have often wondered what she thought about the men I did not marry. Although most of her reactions to my friends, my doings, and my ambitions were clear to me, she never really expressed her opinion of my six men. Perhaps she thought it just as well not to express an opinion, not to sway me in any direction. She certainly did not ever urge me to marry.

From the very beginning she urged my independence. I try to put myself in her position when I, at the age of eight, informed her that I wanted to run a newspaper stand on the street corner. Surely most mothers would have laughed the idea away. But not my mother. The year before, she made the lemonade I offered for sale at two cents a glass near our house; that was a not uncommon childhood enterprise, and even though my only customer was my Aunt Annie, my mother did not suggest I give up business. My father was probably amused by my interest in the selling side of trade, but I think my mother may have felt it was one early step in the direction of female independence. The newsstand was different—now I would be an employee, not the owner—but there is no doubt it was a business undertaking. When I told her about the wondrous ten-cent tip I had been given by a customer, she was as surprised and elated as I was. When I told her I had spent part of the largesse on a peach that had a worm inside, she did not preach but let me draw any moral there might be for myself. And when the family gathered to protest my enterprise and warn her about the child labor laws, she paid no notice and encouraged me to persist. I was doing what I wanted to do and was learning to stand on my own two feet.

Despite the independence she instilled in me, I was still totally dependent upon her. Nothing proved that to me more tellingly than the trip abroad my parents offered me in 1925, when I was just thirteen. It was a "wondrous" trip, but it was a trip with my aunt and my mother's friends, a trip without mother or father. My homesickness centered especially on the absence of my mother, and nothing demonstrates that more pointedly than a poem I wrote to her for her birthday, July 17, when I was aboard the S.S. *Stockholm*, Swedish-America Line, and she was far, far away. Unlike the diary record *My Trip Abroad*, the poem tells the truth of my heart:

> I YEARN FOR YOU, MOTHER, EACH DAY THAT I'M
> AWAY,
> AND NO MATTER WHAT I DO, MY THOUGHTS TO
> YOU WILL STRAY!
> I YEARN FOR YOUR KISS, AND YOUR LOVING SMILE,
> I YEARN TO BE NEAR YOU, JUST FOR A WHILE.
> BUT SEPTEMBER WILL COME; AND DOTH GOD
> PLEASE;
> I SHALL COME WITH IT, YOUR KISS TO SEIZE;
> AND I'LL TELL OF THE COUNTRIES FAR AWAY,
> AND WE'LL BE PALS FOR MANY A DAY.

> BUT, NOW, 'TIS YOUR BIRTHDAY, AND I'D LIKE YOU
> TO KNOW

OF THE THOUGHTS, THAT COULD YOU SEE, WOULD
SHOW
ALL OF LOVE AND JOY FOR YOU,
AND A KISS, AND A WISH, THAT IS NOT NEW,
BUT IT SPEAKS OF JOYS THAT I BEG FROM ABOVE,
TO SHOWER UPON YOU, AND BLESS YOU WITH
LOVE,
FOR YOU KNOW, 'TIS NO MORE THAN YOU JUSTLY
DESERVE,
TO BE BLESSED, AND BE LOVED, AND BY US, TO BE
SERVED.

Did she shed a tear? Did she smile that "loving smile"? Did she sigh when she read my moralistic heartbreaker? I have no idea. All I know is that for the years we would be together, she continued to participate in my life and to serve as a supporting pillar for the castles I tried to build. My mother's life, I realize now, fell into three almost equal segments: the years she spent as a single woman; the years of her marriage; the years of her widowhood. In the last two of those divisions I played a major part. And sometimes, I think, she saw in me and my future the life she herself might have lived.

By 1926, the year of my graduation from junior high school, my mother was truly my companion. One January day, a few weeks before the commencement exercises, she arranged to call for me at school and take me downtown for shopping. Even then I was no enthusiastic shopper, and when she wanted to buy me a dress or a coat, she would promise me a hot fudge sundae at Schrafft's following the purchase. This particular January day turned out to be very special, and I shall never forget it. I think my mother always remembered it, too.

During my last class that day, Miss Presbey, our English teacher, called on me to take a note to the principal's office. As she did so, she whispered to me, "You may read it on your way." As I left the classroom I succumbed immediately to my curiosity and read with a heart-pounding thrill: "The bearer, Miss Madeleine Stern, will receive the Charlton Prize for First Honors at graduation." I could not believe it. It meant that I would be the First Honor girl of 9B, leading the class of students who had completed the first year of high school. It meant that I would deliver the Address of Welcome at graduation. Though I did not know it then, I would receive four additional awards at the upcoming exercises. All that, and now a hot fudge sundae, too.

When my mother picked me up at the side entrance of Joan of Arc Junior High School on West 93rd Street that day, I bubbled and babbled on about the Charlton Prize and the Address of Welcome and Miss Presbey's whisper to read the message. My mother stopped me short. Her words were clear and distinct. "I want to know every single detail. Start from the very beginning. And tell me ALL about it." Now, as I spoke more slowly, I could sense her full and deep participation. She was identifying with me. She was living this with me. I still have the medal for Highest Honor. And I still have the program of Graduation Exercises. But more than any of these, I had and I still have my mother's total empathy.

She was part of so much that I did and thought. She loved words as much as I did, and supplied them often when I needed just the right one to end a verse. She must have transmitted her love of words to me. I remember her pushing a carpet sweeper over a rug and reciting poems or bits of prose at the same time, the words ringing forth to her audience of one. Practically everything I wrote, I read to her in those years before Leona became my sole audience. I even read my master's essay on Mary Magdalene's role in medieval literature to her as I was writing it. She hid very well what must have been her boredom. And then, when most of the finished essay mysteriously disappeared from the Columbia University English Department office, where it was being retyped, she shared my incredulity, my total dismay, my fear that my degree would be withheld, and accompanied me to Morningside Heights to search for the lost pages. The lost pages were never recovered. At the end of the portion that had not been lost I added a footnote about the voluminous section that had been "accidentally destroyed." When my degree was granted despite the strange mishap, my mother rejoiced with me. She cared as much as I did.

Those were the years—the early 1930s—when my mother, my aunt, and I attended the whole repertory of the Theatre Guild, the years when we saw the plays of Arthur Schnitzler and Pirandello, especially of Eugene O'Neill—his *Mourning Becomes Electra,* with dinner between the lengthy acts, and the lovely *Ah, Wilderness!* I had begun work as a teacher-in-training, already taking a mild dislike to it, but I had been able to put aside enough money for a trip abroad. Nothing seemed more natural than to ask my mother if she would make the journey with me.

At the time, when she was in her early sixties, I gave absolutely no thought to any problems or difficulties she might face in traveling abroad with an indefatigable twenty-two-year-old daughter. Especially a daughter consumed with making literary connections and leaving no stones unturned in the process. The journal I kept—a five-year diary devoted to a two-month trip—covered 156 tightly written, numbered pages, to which I added an index. It covers the social customs and eating habits of France and England, the natives I glimpsed, the tourists encountered, the art and architecture, the civilization past and present of my two favorite European countries. However, it makes little if any reference to my mother. I perceived in an American woman seated near us on a bus the reincarnation of Chaucer's prioress, but to the woman seated next to me I gave scarcely a line. Actually, the whole diary should have been dedicated to her.

Fresh from honors in English at Barnard and postgraduate study in medieval literature at Columbia, I sought out literary associations in landscape and gallery; I climbed heights poetical and actual; and my poor mother struggled to keep up. Just before we left Paris for Dinard, the inevitable struck: a crippling attack of sciatica kept her bedridden for days, during which I made a short tour of Brittany and a schematic study of Breton life, all of which I reported to her in lengthy letters. My mother recovered sufficiently to take our journey to England, and there she relished scenes and characters familiar to her from her readings in John Galsworthy and Hugh Walpole family sagas. But keeping up with me was still a challenge, a struggle. Only now has it occurred to me—after all these many years—how well we played the roles of selfless mother and self-centered daughter.

We continued to play those roles during the decade that followed. Protective supporter of me and my enterprises, mainstay of our household, domestic genie, my mother filled her free time reading books and playing heated games of bridge with her cronies. I do not recall a single occasion when she did not have time for me—time to welcome me home from teaching, time to listen to my latest poem or essay, time to discuss my friends. It was during these years that Leona became not only my closest friend but my mother's number one favorite. She had little to volunteer about my other companions; at best, they were "all right," at worst, she was "not crazy about any of them." But Leona soon became her "Leonchen," her "little Leona," whom she would grow to love almost as much as I would.

In those years before we entered World War II, I was researching my *Life of Margaret Fuller* during trips to Boston and Concord, during more trips to the New York Public Library. When I decided to end my research and start the actual writing, she sat down to listen to my readings, to comment briefly but always honestly. When she thought a phrase or paragraph was good, she said so, and I felt that was high praise. With me she lived through the crises inevitable in a first biography, and with me she rejoiced at the endorsements from the distinguished literary critic Van Wyck Brooks. When E. P. Dutton accepted the work for publication, my mother, Leona, and I celebrated at the White Turkey Inn near Danbury, and when, in January 1942, just after our country had entered World War II, my book received a glowing first-page review in the *Herald Tribune,* she exulted almost as much as I did.

Leona—"Leonchen"—my mother and I had become a threesome by the 1940s. We played canasta together and kept a "kitty," saving the nickels and dimes we lost at the game for future treats. A typical treat consisted of a movie—perhaps *Jane Eyre* or *Casablanca* or almost any performance at Radio City Music Hall—followed by dinner at a nearby Longchamps or Schrafft's restaurant. Sometimes we varied the program with a bite at Lindy's, a popular eating place named after the famous flier.

That pattern persisted after the revolutionary act that changed my career and my life in the spring of 1945. During the years when I had progressed from teacher-in-training to substitute teacher and finally to permanent or tenured teacher, my attitude toward the profession had deteriorated. I found myself less and less interested in pedagogical arts and increasingly eager to devote myself to writing. Actually, I had written my *Life of Margaret Fuller* and done much of the research for my biography of Louisa May Alcott during my time as a teacher. But it was an exhausting combination. In 1944, after her five years of apprenticeship, Leona founded the firm of Leona Rostenberg—Rare Books, in which I already felt deeply involved. Earlier I had been awarded a Guggenheim Fellowship to work on the Alcott biography, and my life as a "Guggenheim" spoiled me forever for a return to teaching. The taste of freedom was addictive, and I wanted more of it—more elasticity, more command of my life. I had long dreamed of joining Leona in her rare book business. She had rekindled in me my love of antiquarian books; working with her would give me freedom of choice, time to pursue my scholarly interests, and the delight of having her companionship continuously.

A brief return to teaching at the termination of my Guggenheim decided me. My life lay with the

promising rare book firm created by Leona Rostenberg—not with the city school system. On April 9,
1945, I resigned my enviable tenured position, and,
when I returned home, informed my mother tersely,
without explanation, what I had done. I did not
dream of putting myself in her place when she heard
the words: "I resigned today from teaching." Teaching, we both knew, brought me a steady, decent income in 1945. I had tenure, which meant then a
certain and secure future. Teaching conditions, if not
perfect, involved no anxiety about safety in those
days. It was what was called the perfect profession
for a single woman. Now I was giving it all up. My
mother's immediate response was, "Something terrible must have happened!" to which I replied with reference less to the annoyances that had assailed me
than to my long-term and growing distaste for teaching and my equally long-term and growing desire to
become an active partner in Leona Rostenberg—Rare
Books. If my mother was troubled about my future,
as she must assuredly have been, she did not share her
concern with me. The deed was done and could not
and would not be undone. My mother was a realist

who still believed that I must live my own life. Now I would live it. She would continue to stand by me.

She would continue, too, to share and delight in the successes of Leona Rostenberg—Rare Books. During the years that followed, we restocked our shelves annually by trips, often extended ones, abroad. My mother participated in those trips through her letters, faithfully dispatched to us a few times a week. I kept them all, and they make a sizable collection. They serve, too, as indicators of her realistic attitude toward her own life and her unceasing exultation in all our coups. There is no palaver in her letters. But there is strong support and deep love. A few excerpts reflect her image between 1947, when we made our first trans-Atlantic book-buying venture, and 1958, when she died.

A letter sent to us in 1947, directed to the Pension Iris in Interlaken, where we were taking a brief vacation, began, as all my mother's letters did, "Darling" or "Darling Madeleine." It expresses the hope that we will "continue getting books," and it comments: "It is really marvelous that you succeeded in getting so many treasures in such a short time." She was right. During our 1947 search we purchased 280 books, most of them from a London still war-torn after the Blitz. My mother's letter, direct and straightforward, goes on to outline her activities: the people she saw, the food she ate, her winnings or losings at rummy, bridge, or Scrabble, a movie seen. Always she mentioned that she had spoken on the phone to the Rostenbergs or seen them, and she assured us that "all is fine up there." She too was fine—no need for us to fret about anything, and she signed off with "lots of love to both" from Mother.

What change there was in my mother's letters during the years that followed was a reflection of the change in Leona's life. Her father died in 1950, and during the next seven years, the two mothers grew especially close. My mother's letters abroad reported her weekly trips uptown to see her widowed friend. Those visits and the reports of them ended in 1957, with the death of Leona's mother.

Otherwise my mother's letters through those years did not change noticeably. She was still hoping we would enjoy our sessions with booksellers and that we would get more books at our next port of call. She was still assuring us that all was well with her. And she was still signing off "with all my love to both" from Mother. Very occasionally in 1957 she would include a slightly uncharacteristic thought: "Just about half of the time that you'll be away has passed. . . . I am sure the next half will pass quickly."

In 1958 we postponed our departure for the book hunt several times because of my mother's ailing health. She died on August 26. We left finally in September. There were no letters from her that year.

LEONA

Although our mothers' life spans were almost identical, Lillie Stern's life fell into three segments, my mother's into only two. She was the single Louisa Dreyfus till she was thirty-two. For most of her remaining years she was the wife, Mrs. Adolph Rostenberg. The first part of her life was dominated by her place of birth, New Orleans. The second part was dominated in large part by me.

My mother's all-consuming love for me was returned in full measure. I believe now that her love for me was a compensation for a not altogether satisfactory marriage. There is little doubt in my mind that my mother at the age of thirty-two accepted my father's hand as a compromise. There were vast differences in background and in character between them. The Southern belle would surely have preferred an American husband, and at her age would also have preferred a more mature, less demanding mate. It was predictable that, with her somewhat snobbish nature, she would have found life in the Bronx socially disastrous. With the birth of a son and, three years later, a little girl, and the experience of watching the children develop, her loving, caring nature centered less on husband than on children, and, in time, less on son than on daughter.

As for me, I adored my mother from my earliest years. At first I loved above all the way she looked. Her features were so aesthetically appealing that I could linger on them in admiration. Her eyes danced winningly, flirtatiously. She moved with a rhythmic beauty. It was not long before I discovered—or believed—that she was everything I was not. From the age of two I had to wear eyeglasses, and though they were attached to my ears with ribbon and not metal sidepieces, they were, to me at least, a peculiar deformity. I had inherited my father's features and felt they were far inferior to hers. In my besotted eyes, she was beauty—I, the little girl with eyeglasses. As a result, I withdrew, and my shyness increased for all the world, except for Mother.

With her I was able to invert our roles, helping her in her need. I still have a letter dated November 25, 1915, written by my mother to my father, who was visiting his parents in Pittsburgh. "Dearest Schatz" [Treasure], she called him, and told him of her worry about his safe arrival. She added that her "precious" little girl was "so comforting, acting like a little mother in her solicitude." I was then not yet seven. My own note to my father confirms all this: "I took care of momma last night. She called me her little mother."

The next summer, at Chebeaque Island off the coast of Maine, where the family sought refuge from the polio epidemic, I continued my maternal role. When my mother went rowing with a Canadian visitor, I chided her, "Remember you're a married woman." When she picked up a cigarette, I admonished her, "I don't think you should smoke." Little Miss Morality could take the lead with Mother but with no one else.

Despite my air of authority with her, my mother was not at all confident about my seeming maturity. Around this time my elementary school teacher, Miss Greenberg, informed me that I was skipping, entering 3A instead of 2B. My mother went to school immediately to discuss this giant step. She questioned whether I was sufficiently developed to enter an advanced class. I was so small, so shy.

Nonetheless, I did skip. I held my own in school. But I did not shed my shyness. I was still withdrawn. I found myself only in relation to my mother. Three years later, my adoration for her persisted. My parents were off to Pittsburgh, and a letter I sent to them in 1918, a day after my tenth birthday, attests to this:

> *Hello Sweethearts,*
> *. . . Well well how was a nights sleep on a pulmer [Pullman]. How is karfilter [gefühlte] fish. I myself had to go down to the drug-store to get Master Tuck Rostenberg [the*

dog] a bottle of Castor-oil. Sweethearts I am terribly homesick. The moment you left Joy was turned to sorrow. And Mammy darling your sweet looks are in my thoughts both day and night. . . . I am going now to play with the children. So I must end my little letter. . . . Love and kisses From your loving little daughter Leona.

The emotional tie between "loving little daughter" and mother darling grew only closer as time passed. At camp, the only public school girl from the Bronx attracted admiration because of her difference and became acceptable and even exotic to the snobs from Manhattan. My popularity at Camp Kearsage helped me lose my shyness. At the same time, my mother missed me so acutely that she took off for Lake Sebago to spend a few days alone with her daughter. The bond between us strengthened.

Unlike Madeleine's mother, my mother did not lend support at every crucial stage of my life. Unlike Madeleine's mother, who spent a third of her life as a widow, my mother was, until her later years, a wife, the wife of a physician, with all the obligations this entailed. She had many interests, many responsibilities, and as I grew older, I began to realize that she was not mine alone. To aid and abet her husband, she served as president of the ladies' auxiliary in his hospital, a time-consuming task. As a wife, she organized dinner parties for my father's colleagues. She lost none of her beauty or charm as she aged, and she was much in demand for all sorts of social occasions, from bridge parties to fund-raising ceremonies. She loved to shop. She loved clothes, and the wardrobe she assembled enhanced her loveliness. She could even be induced to recite at some of the gatherings she attended. Madeleine's mother may have recited to an audience of Madeleine, but my mother often entranced a large assemblage. She had never forgotten her elocution lessons in New Orleans or, early in her married life, her thwarted ambition to act on stage.

I shared my mother with my father, with my brother, with her friends, with her own concerns and pleasures. But I never questioned the love she showered on me. For me, being loved by her was compensation for my doubts and self-seeking. Her love enveloped me in warmth and gave me strength. Writing in my diary in the 1930s, I tried to analyze the nature of that love: "Mother . . . is soft, loving—too generous—never finding fault—*spoiling* & praising me. Gentle."

Nothing epitomizes more acutely the difference between Madeleine's mother and mine than the letters they sent to us when we traveled abroad. Where Madeleine's mother wrote forthright and direct notes about her doings and ours, my mother loosed her emotional reins and deluged me with her feelings. I have saved nearly all of them, but this one will suffice:

> *I'd give anything to hold my Doll just for a few seconds, how gladly I conquer my desire in the thought that our temporary separation brings to fruition your dream of accomplishment.*

References to the "vast distance" between us, her "fantastic imagination" that makes her "visualize the most dreadful situations" follow, and she ends by confessing to me that "It is all I think of—during the day and the many sleepless hours at night."

How different they were, those two mothers whose loving shaped our lives.

My father died suddenly of a heart attack in 1950. My mother lived on another seven years, at first in a slow, almost imperceptible decline. As she approached her eighties, she lost most of her sight. As a result of her disability, her need of me strengthened. Although I loved her so deeply, I felt the silver cord tighten. Now she spent hours listening to phonograph records of novels like *Came a Cavalier,* stories that recalled to her the dreams of her youth. She listened too to my reports of the development of our young business. During a book hunt abroad with Madeleine in 1956, I received word from our beloved housekeeper that my mother had collapsed and was calling constantly for me.

The following year I did not have to worry about going abroad and leaving her. My mother left me on March 13, 1957.

Les Femmes Militaires [Militant Women].
Louis Rustaing de Saint-Jory, French, 1739

An illustrated utopian romance set in America, proclaiming absolute parity of men and women in work, government service, war and life. With engraved frontispiece and five full-page plates depicting women in military costume, etc. Bound in calf.

*Acquired by Yale University
Library, 1948*

Chapter Five

TWO BOOK WOMEN
IN A MAN'S WORLD

The house that was now Leona's embraced us both but never confined or constrained us. It was a loving, loose embrace. The house had always had that quality, that power. From the beginning, it had stood, a sprawling country cottage, in the midst of a borough that was quickly being urbanized, citified. Its three stories and attic, the lower stories belted with comfortable porches, had been for Leona a certainty in an uncertain world. In its little garden an apple tree flaunted its blossoms, its perfume, every spring. The house had been witness to all her travails and triumphs. It had welcomed the German housekeeper, Babette, who found refuge there from her troubled German world. Almost at the same time Babette arrived, lonely and insecure, Adolph, Jr., found a frightened mongrel with a rope around his neck and

159

introduced him to the ménage. Having found a haven, the two newcomers comforted each other and, in turn, added comfort and security to the big house. Babette stayed on, witnessing changes without and within, the departure of Adolph, Jr., the death of Adolph, Sr., the antics of Leona and her friend Madeleine, the succession of pets—a rabbit at one time, a canary at another, but always the dogs, loved and loving. It had always been a place of roots, a place for abiding.

And now it was our turn. Now Madeleine brought her own lares and penates to the house, and the house included them in its embrace. The lovely octagonal room overlooking 179th Street, once a doctor's consulting room, was transformed into Madeleine's office. There she brought her bookcases and her files, her notes for the book she was working on in 1958, and the supplies she would need as partner in Leona Rostenberg—Rare Books. Upstairs, up the graceful, curving staircase with the grandfather's clock at the turn, on the second floor, the large luxurious bedroom that had been Leona's parents' was now Madeleine's. The house was filled with light and air, with warmth and love. For us two, together now, it was our anchor in a shifting world.

For more than thirty years it had been a safe harbor for Leona. She had returned to it from school to find a sure retreat. If she felt shy or lonely, it gave her a sense of belonging. She was never shy or lonely within those walls. There, she had grown up, faced her problems, searched for selfhood, discussed with her father, confided in her mother, rejoiced in her friendship with Madeleine. When she began her antiquarian business, she converted the bedroom vacated by her brother into an office that boasted the first stock of Leona Rostenberg—Rare Books, a stock of thirty books. In 1957 Leona inherited that sprawling country house, and then she was able to renovate it, giving it a second life.

After Madeleine's arrival the following year, the two friends would embark upon their own second life. The big house would become the background for an even closer companionship, as well as for an expanded business—the bulwark of two women acting out their lives in a man's world.

The house seemed to expand itself for us. Dr.

Rostenberg's enormous examination room now became our packing room, our unpacking room, our
examination room. With every trip abroad we took
to hunt for books, more and more packages were
piled up there. They bore a colorful array of return
addresses, most of them in London and Paris, but as
the years passed, the nations enriching our bookshelves came to include Italy and the Netherlands,
Austria and Germany, far-off Japan. As soon as we
returned from our journeys, we would hasten to the
packing room to retrieve a bundle or two, unwrap
them in eager haste, check and collate our findings,
scan the pages, read between the lines, ponder the political pronouncements in our seventeenth-century
French pamphlets, glory in the portraits that illustrated our eighteenth-century biographical antholo-
gies, search every tract and volume for a previously
unnoticed reference to the New World or a new in-
vention or a fresh idea. Out of the packing room
came our disappointments and our exultations, especially our discoveries.

Then, into the packing room went the results of
our labors—the books that had been offered to and

ordered by our collectors and librarians. Carefully we wrapped them in white tissue paper, encased them next in corrugated paper cut to their measure, and finally secured them in brown wrapping paper, ready for the post. Dr. Rostenberg's examination room had become our in-and-out room, the genesis and exodus of our bookselling testament.

Upstairs, on the third floor, we established what might well be called our waiting room or holding room. There, where Adolph, Jr.'s Ping-Pong table had once dominated, we placed several bookcases and filled them with books on reserve. In the course of the decade, until 1969, when we made our move to Manhattan, we stored our collections there until we felt the time had come to catalogue them and offer them for *en bloc* purchase. In that huge upstairs room, our sixteenth- and seventeenth-century French pamphlets awaited us until they formed the basis of a documentary history of France between 1550 and 1650, as well as the French Revolutionary pamphlets that would bring to life a country's hopes and agonies, the turmoil of anarchy, the search for the rights of man, the terror of the guillotine. In special grandeur stood our collection of Aldines, those volumes that issued from the Venetian press of a great publishing family between 1494 and 1595 and incidentally provided the classics in portable format so that those who ran might read. Finally, the third-floor room held in waiting our collection of books by and about another great Italian family, the Medicis of Florence, whose influence extended in colorful grandeur through much of Europe. All four collections would be described and sold *en bloc* and thus make possible our eventual move to Manhattan.

Now, that was a long way off. Now, we were earning the description of us that appeared in a directory of *Book Dealers in North America* as "a well-known New York dealer who operates from the Bronx." Now, we were developing a business together, expanding it, enlarging our horizons. The word "together" looms as the most important one in this context, and most of our business contacts seemed well aware of it. One would write to Leona, after chatting with us at a book fair: "The personality of yourself and your partner, Ms. Stern, blend in perfectly as one." According to another, "Your joint scholarship and friendship is a union of marvels and erudition," while a third summed up simply, "I always think of the two of you as a team." The team was a team of working women in what was still a man's world.

It was a world that we took for granted. It was part of the climate of the time, and we expected it. Leona recalled all too well the calm, clear statement of fact made to her by a Columbia University professor when she had attended graduate school: "Don't set your sights too high, Miss Rostenberg. Remember, you are a woman and a Jew." To which Miss Rostenberg had replied, "There is nothing I can do about either." Just as the 10 percent Jewish quota had been an unquestioned tradition when Madeleine was at Barnard, there seemed to be an unwritten quota that applied to women who tried to survive in a business world dominated by men. Margaret Fuller might have demanded for her sex, "Let them be sea-captains, if you will," but few if any had listened. Entering certain trades and professions was still a struggle, and equal pay for equal work was the same will-o'-the-wisp it had been in the nineteenth century. As a matter of fact, Madeleine was at this very time working on a biographical anthology about the women who had opened up a variety of "male" occupations to their sex. But not one had been a dealer in antiquarian books.

When we entered the field, we had been preceded by a few other pioneers, but the proportion of women to men was still minimal. We had been accepted as members of our association, the Antiquarian Booksellers Association of America, and at its early meetings we invariably sat together in silence in the rear of the hall, a practice that inspired one macho male to comment scornfully, "What's the matter—are you afraid to separate?" During its first quarter century that male-dominated association could boast only two women presidents, one of whom would be Leona Rostenberg.

Male chauvinism dominated other book associations even more noticeably. The Grolier Club, the most prestigious group of bibliophiles in the country, named after a great sixteenth-century collector, simply did not accept women members. When, years later, the club was forced to change its exclusionary ruling, we tentatively inquired about the procedures for applying for admission. By then we had gained a wide reputation as respected members of the book trade, but the secretary's response was, "You will have to prove that you have a genuine interest in books." The secretary, of course, was a male, and we never did present our bookish credentials to him or to his successors.

It was scarcely remarkable that within the Grolier Club at the time there was another, equally male-dominated group known as the Old Book Table. Once, during Leona's presidency of the Antiquarian Booksellers Association of America, we were invited for dinner, and the table talk was free of male chauvinism. However, we often wondered what sort of conversation went on there when these two feminists were not present.

We countered the attitude of this man's world in several ways. One Christmas we had imprinted a greeting card that read on its cover: "PEACE ON EARTH GOOD WILL TOWARD MEN . . ." and on the inside fold the message continued: "AND WOMEN." We were later informed that one copy, sent to a New

York Public Library curator, was filed in the library's Ephemera Collection devoted to "Women's suffrage and liberation."

Our fighting consisted for the most part in pioneering. We simply carried on, as a team, in this man's world. We were especially interested in amassing, cataloguing, selling, and lecturing on "Books By and About Feminists." For each of us it was a fascinating revelation to discover how long ago women had begun to express themselves in manuscript or in print. Improbable though it seemed, it was as long ago as the fourth century that a bluestocking named Falconia Proba rearranged the lines of Virgil's *Aeneid* to narrate the stories of the Bible. Her *Centones* became the very first composition by a woman to be printed—surely a landmark for any feminist library. The copy we found, printed in 1513, had been owned by one of the few male champions of women, a German publisher named Jacob Koebel. We sold the prize to Miriam Y. Holden, who was building one of the earliest and best feminist libraries and who became not only a faithful customer but a faithful friend. By the sixteenth century, the weaker sex was actively demonstrating its strength in publications that reflected its learning and intellectual egalitarianism, not to mention its role in the flowering of the Renaissance. In France, there was the extraordinary Louise Labé, who—truly a woman in the military—fought at the Siege of Perpignan, gathered the Lyonese society around her, and wrote charming verses.

Such women writers were remarkable, but both we and our collectors were far more interested in the militant literature produced by women of later centuries. An anonymous *Serious Proposal to the Ladies . . . By a Lover of Her Sex* appeared in 1694 and was ascribed to Mary Astell. It contained the germ of the modern woman's college. In the eighteenth century, Mary Wollstonecraft gave us her *Vindication of the Rights of Woman,* and in the nineteenth, Margaret Fuller, whose biography Madeleine wrote and who had pleaded for women to be sea captains or anything else they wished to be, was a natural catch for our net, and we acquired copies of *Woman in the Nineteenth Century* whenever we could.

At one of our association's annual Book Fairs,

we presented a small but significant collection of feminist books that caught the eye of a *Times* reporter, who described its highlights: "An 18th-century French tract favoring divorce; two works on Pope Joan; two works on Joan of Arc; the first American edition of John Stuart Mill's 1869 feminist landmark, 'The Subjection of Women,' a feminist Who's Who of 1879 in French, and the 1792 edition of Mary Wollstonecraft's *Vindication of the Rights of Woman.*"

We did more than buy and sell such books. We tried to spread the word that these women authors had planted seeds, many of which have yet to flower. We traveled across much of the country, lecturing on those books, and we called our lecture "Feminism Is Collectible." It turned out to be a popular subject indeed, and it was delivered—sometimes by the two of us in tandem—at a succession of universities and schools of library science. Often there was standing room only for those talks on feminist books, and reactions were heartwarming. One we savored the most was from a male publisher. It was a question, but it was followed by an exclamation point: "Why must women have all the brains!"

One of our major discoveries relating to literature as well as to gender was made together. The story has become well known, but it is sufficiently exciting to bear repeating. In the course of research for Madeleine's biography of Louisa May Alcott, we worked together at Harvard's Houghton Library. There Leona, sifting through stacks of manuscripts, pounced upon five letters from a Boston publisher revealing the staggering information that "Dear Miss Alcott" had used the pseudonym A. M. Barnard to write unacknowledged thrillers with such alluring feminist titles as "Behind a Mask: or, A Woman's Power" and "A Marble Woman: or, The Mysterious Model."

The discovery, which we gloried in, started us on the track of more such narratives by "Dear Miss Alcott," and in due course we found them, flipping through the pages of such sensational nineteenth-century periodicals as *The Flag of Our Union* and *Frank Leslie's Illustrated Newspaper.* What Leona started, Madeleine finished, editing half a dozen collections of thrilling tales, many with a feminist slant, penned in secret by the "Children's Friend" and published anonymously or pseudonymously. The research was ours, and so were the joys of discovery, the experience of two twentieth-century feminists working in tandem.

Feminism was only one of the subjects we tried to develop for librarians and collectors and to publicize for any who would listen. Knowledgeable aficionados in love with Renaissance books made a great audience for our talks about the great Aldine Press of Venice, but there was seldom an empty seat when we spoke on the subject of ephemera. As we believed, "to study and reanimate the past, scholars need to know the past when the past was the present." And what could reanimate the past more vividly than its printed records in the form of pamphlets read and thrown away, nailed to walls and blown away. We looked for them everywhere, buying them individually or in small collections—especially those ephemera in French that had been printed in the sixteenth and seventeenth centuries to air views popular or controversial, to comment upon the need for civil rights and religious freedom, to reflect the conflicts and the pacts of a tumultuous time—pamphlets that gave us a collective memory of past centuries. Our audiences were usually enthralled.

We talked about such "Uncommon Collectibles" and the sleuthing that had uncovered them all across the country, from Asbury Park to Binghamton, from Baltimore to Milwaukee, from North Carolina to Indiana, from Albany, New York, to Provo, Utah, from the Brotherhood of Temple Emanu-El in Yonkers, New York, to Messiah College in Grantham, Pennsylvania. All sorts of audiences were captivated by the idea of analyzing historical pamphlets that recorded great events, from Columbus' discovery of America to the California gold rush. And we advised them in our codas: "Search in the present and the future. Visualize all the ephemera that will fill your mailboxes or be passed to you on street corners. . . . Among them there will be some slips of paper that turn a political tide or reconstruct a historic moment. Their recognition and their preservation will make you all discoverers."

Together we entrained and enplaned to deliver our message. Together we catalogued our findings. Today, when we reread those catalogue descriptions, we seldom know which one of us wrote which. At board meetings attended by the two partners and their incumbent pet, we decided who would work on what. Leona was always assigned the historical and political volumes; Madeleine, the literary and artistic. All the German books went to Leona; many of the French to Madeleine. The division of subject came as naturally as our lives together. We met frequently in our reference room, but we wrote our descriptions separately in our individual studies. Prefaces and forewords were written in duo. Madeleine did the indexes and proofreading. We transported the finished catalogues to the post office together, always in high hope and anticipation.

Soon after Madeleine's move to the Bronx house, we purchased a car, a blue Rambler, in which we drove not only to the post office but to points beyond. We drove, for example, to the Manhattan hotels where our collectors or librarians were staying for their book hunts in New York, and we conveyed such prospective customers to what was to them the remote Borough of the Bronx. Like us, they reveled in the spacious house that seemed to have room for everything, and they usually selected books on the grand scale.

It was a time of growth and expansion for us, and the growth continued after our move in 1969 to

Manhattan. It was no longer necessary for us then to convey our customers to our place of business; they could find their way themselves. And they did. The results of our efforts were taking very tangible form, and most of them came from the men in this man's world.

The results manifested themselves at first in the letters we received. When our earliest collaboration, *Old & Rare,* was published in 1974, reading it, according to *Publishers Weekly,* was "a bit like listening to Beethoven's 'Ode to Joy.'" Readers seemed to agree, for their comments about this joint reminiscence of our antiquarian career flowed in from a world-wide web, from Wichita, Kansas, to Calgary, Canada, from the Canary Islands to Ahmedabad, India. Through the years the letters brightened our mail. Pleas for advice from ambitious, book-loving scholars in South Bend, Indiana, who asked us whether they should enter the rare book trade, vied with letters from established colleagues, one of whom wrote: "I am a more knowledgeable bookseller because of your many published contributions. Not only are they scholarly, but there is always a humorous vein throughout." Another, a bookseller in Vaduz, Liechtenstein, addressed us as "Dear Colleagues, adored ladies." Needless to say, both were men. Rostenberg and Stern were being referred to now as the "doyennes" of American antiquarian bookselling. Our pride in the appellation dimmed a bit when we checked the dictionary and learned that doyennes were characterized more by seniority than by anything else.

It was certainly in part thanks to seniority that we were developing a substantial reputation in the trade. A newspaper account of a prestigious auction noted that Leona Rostenberg was one of a dozen "men" who were the strongest purchasers at a New York sale, and Christie's in Canada informed Leona that they had taken the liberty to refer to her as the bibliographical authority regarding the Aldine. At a New York Book Fair where we exhibited, a couple singled the firm out as "the most delightful bookseller duo," a "redoubtable team."

The "redoubtable team" was interviewed now for radio and TV appearances, along with newspaper features, which they happily clipped and pasted into scrapbooks. When one *New York Times* article traced our beginnings from the imprinted stationery Madeleine had presented to Leona, a colleague observed that such publicity was a "lovely boost for the rare book business and woman's lib all in one rare combination." Suddenly it seemed as if we too were becoming collectible. An archive of our records and writings that we deposited in the Harold B. Lee Library of Brigham Young University in Utah elicited the following encomium from the librarian, Dean Larsen: "The Stern & Rostenberg collections . . . have grown in magnitude; and are, indeed, becoming research collections for future scholars." We have recently been memorialized in the *Dictionary of Literary Biography,* where the author Ruth Rosenberg sums up: "Their legacy to posterity is to have served as trustees of civilization through the mastery of their profession."

All this is indeed very gratifying, but somehow we are not yet ready to be trustees or dispensers of a legacy. We have always loved what we do, and so we want to continue doing what we love. There are obstacles to such continuance, however, that we must face if we hope to make ourselves felt as before. The principal obstacle, of course, is time—time that changes us, but more particularly time that changes our world. Either we join that transformed world or we leave it. Either we take up the challenge of the newness or accept the role of legator. We study our books before we dispose of them. Just so, we must study our changing world before we can decide our fate.

Old & Rare: Forty Years in the Book Business, Leona Rostenberg and Madeleine B. Stern, 1988

A chapter was added to this second revised edition of the co-authors' comments on the book trade. Entitled "Changing Blueprint," it offers thoughts on transformations in dealers' attitudes, collectors' goals, and antiquarian bookselling at home and abroad. Paperback.

Still in print

Chapter Six
OUR CHANGING BOOK WORLD

We can now, in this new millennium, look back over nearly one hundred years. It is a staggering thought. The first half of the twentieth century was our inheritance, and its changing attitudes and practices colored much of the second half, in which we were actors. We can truthfully testify to the incredible transformations that have shaped and reshaped that best and worst of times.

We are especially equipped to report the changes in one small area of the twentieth century—the area where booksellers sell their wares and libraries and collectors buy them. In 1947, when we returned from our first antiquarian book hunt abroad, we felt that, having looked through windows from which the stained glass had been stricken, we had seen and been part of the most cataclysmic of changed worlds. We knew then that, though we would return to Europe many, many times, and see the rebuilding after World War II, the transitions, the newness, that particular world we would never see again. In some ways we feel now, at the end of our century, that the antiquarian book world so long our familiar background is also a lost shadow. Certainly we shall never see it again as it once was. Like some of the books we have bought, it has become *introuvable.*

In order to convey the nature and extent of the changes we have witnessed in our trade, we must say a word about how it was when we began. Its setting, its cast of characters were quite different. The bibliopolic play in which we were beginning actors had different conventions and was performed for a different audience.

As apprentice to the refugee rare book dealer Herbert Reichner, Leona was heir to much that had gone before. Incidentally, by now the concepts of both apprentice and refugee dealer have disappeared from the scene, as have so many other aspects of the antiquarian business. A day in the life of apprentice Leona depicts a day in another age. The day began punctually at nine A.M., and the week consisted of six days. Her employer was a refugee from Austria, and her conversation with him was often in German. Like many other refugee dealers escaping the ravages of Adolf Hitler, Herbert Reichner embodied the classical tradition, which included a knowledge of Latin and Greek and a familiarity with early printed books. Such books surrounded Leona as she worked in his office on New York's East 62nd Street: incunabula, or books produced from the "cradle" of printing by movable type, books always learned, often devout, sometimes profound, and frequently most handsome, illustrated with early woodcuts, bound in vellum or pigskin over boards, books of knowledge, books of beauty.

Leona's apprenticeship introduced her to librarians and collectors who were steeped in the same classical tradition. They called at Reichner's office: Lessing Rosenwald from Jenkintown, Pennsylvania, in search of incunabula; Philip Hofer from Harvard looking for sixteenth-century illustrated books; Harrison Horblit ferreting out early texts in science; the legendary librarian William A. Jackson seeking volumes for Harvard's bookshelves; the colorful Hungarian Zoltan Haraszti buying Renaissance folios for the Boston Public Library. When Rachel Hunt arrived from her estate in Pennsylvania, Leona—never more than four feet ten inches tall—was instructed to hold the ladder while she climbed up to the highest shelf in search of botanical rarities for her library. They came with knowledge and understanding, those collectors, knowing what they wanted, eager, filled with zest and excitement.

Fellow dealers also dropped in on Herbert Reichner and his apprentice. There were, of course, numerous other refugee dealers who, like Reichner, brought their continental tastes and classical learning to the American rare book trade, enriching it beyond measure. And there were the highly educated American dealers too, their names now awesome in the trade: Dr. A.S.W. Rosenbach from Philadelphia, familiarly known as Dr. R; the erudite New Yorker Lathrop Harper—both staunch pillars of a prestigious trade. Lathrop Harper went way back. He had known the Leon brothers, who in 1885 issued the first catalogue of American first editions, and later on, when

Madeleine was researching the Leons, she consulted the distinguished Mr. Harper. The dealers, like the collectors, were for the most part men of learning, connoisseurs, and scholars. Indeed, in the pages of *The New York Times Book Review* their exploits could be followed, for there Philip Brooks conducted a column on rare books, reporting coups at auction and the highlights of dealers' catalogues.

Although the dealers of old were strongly individualistic, sometimes to the point of eccentricity, it is possible to create an imaginary profile that conveys their characteristics. He—all the major dealers were male—probably hailed from the eastern United States and had to his credit at least four years at an Ivy League college and a few years of graduate study. He was familiar with Latin, if not Greek, and fluent in at least one or two foreign tongues. Having either a small private income or the benefit of some trust fund, he could indulge his awakening interest in collecting books, especially the books he had studied in the languages in which they had originally appeared. In the course of his periodic visits abroad, he explored not only the Bodleian Library and the British

Museum, but those fascinating spots where books were sold, from the modest bookstalls of Paris's Left Bank to the London establishment of Bernard Quaritch. Then, disenchanted after a stint at law school or even a year or so with a prestigious banking house, our Mr. X decided to indulge his now fully developed passion for books and join the bibliopolic profession. He would devote his life to the purchase, the study, and the sale of the early printed book.

The booktrade of the 1940s that Leona witnessed as a young apprentice differed from the booktrade of the 1990s in yet another major aspect: its methods of communication. Orders that arrived in Mr. Reichner's office came from abroad by cable or by post. Domestic orders came by post, Western Union telegram, or telephone. When Mr. Reichner's catalogues were distributed, the mail orders lined the floor, and the phone never stopped ringing. With frenzied enthusiasm books in the classical tradition were sought; esoteric tomes in Greek and Latin as well as in foreign languages were amassed. For better or for worse, it was a different world.

When we first became partners in the rare book

business, we were of course unaware of that. We thought the world in which Leona had studied and apprenticed would last forever. We ourselves were still too young to realize that such a conviction is always a delusion. It was probably not till the end of the 1960s that we became fully aware of the spirit of change at work in our world. Earlier on, it had been a foregone conclusion that our customers had at least a working knowledge of one or more foreign languages, and we busily stocked our shelves with books on the literature, the history, and the political institutions of seventeenth- and eighteenth-century France and Italy, for example, written in the languages of those countries—books that could reanimate an earlier time and a distant place, provided, of course, that their readers knew some French and Italian. But as the 1960s rolled on in their tumultuous course, customers browsing our shelves for the first time began to shy away from the "foreign stuff" and ask, "Don't you have anything in English? We're interested in foreign countries, but we'd like to read about them in translation." Soon an English translation of a pamphlet on the execution of Marie Antoinette, which formerly had been shunned by collectors seeking the original French version, came to be preferred to the original. It occurred to us that if we stubbornly persisted in our selections of books in foreign tongues, we might soon need to look for customers.

It did not take us long to understand the reason for this particular change in collecting taste. Customers trained in the classical heritage, adept in European languages, were dying out, being replaced by a newer, younger, differently educated breed. Either we adapted to their demands or we stopped selling books. There was no doubt in our minds that it was the American system of education that was primarily responsible for this transformation in rare book collecting. The high school and college curricula included practically no Greek, very little Latin, and as for foreign languages, Spanish might be available, but neither French nor Italian was highlighted. We were aware that every generation finds fault with the curricula offered the next generation. Had not Leona's father exploded in outrage when he learned that Greek was not available to his daughter at Evander Childs High School? The collectors Leona had met at

Reichner's, trained in the classics, were thinning out, being replaced by collectors less in the European than the almost chauvinistic American tradition. We had to attract them now to our bookshelves.

There were other reasons for the change in collecting taste. People had less space for books than they had formerly had. Mansions with one or more rooms whose paneled walls held mahogany shelves for books were being razed, and in their place tighter apartments were being rented, apartments that had no space for libraries. Many of our younger collectors had far less money than the collectors of old. Less space, less money, and a different education added up to a new type of collector, one who preferred first editions of English and American literature, especially "modern firsts" with crisp printed jackets, to the elephant folios issued during the Renaissance. The collecting of rare books was being, in a word, democratized, and who could find fault with democratization no matter what form it took?

College and university libraries reflected the shift in interest. Our old librarian friends who had invited us to build collections for them on the work of humanistic freethinkers like Etienne Dolet or foreign patrons of learning like the Medicis now turned to assembling books on the British succession, the American frontier, nineteenth-century feminists, or contemporary writing. Since a large percentage of our business was done with the libraries of our country, we had, perforce, to take their altered emphases into consideration. For us it was not "Publish or Perish" but "Adapt or Perish."

Our younger colleagues, who had never known the world in which we began, were adept at supplying desiderata to their customers. They themselves represented a new breed of dealer. Here is our imaginary profile of Mr. X's descendant, the current dispenser of antiquarian books, whom we shall call "Y." Such a profile will throw into focus the changes we have noticed in the trade in general and perhaps a few others too. Hailing from the western states rather than the east, Y formed a strong contrast to X. Unlike X, Y probably originated in California, where he or she— Y was as likely to be Ms. as Mr.—spent perhaps two years at a community college. Y's education stressed the practical rather than the aesthetic and included little if any training in foreign languages. School was followed by a stint in stock brokerage or more likely in computers, where Y was able to earn a sizable fund of money. How to spend it was the problem, not how to earn it. Reading about the astronomical prices paid at auction for books and manuscripts, Y began to look upon such objects as merchandise for sale or investment. Soon, browsing in bookstores or keeping abreast of auctions, Y developed a lively interest in such subjects as jazz and blues, Beat literature, or constructivism—provided the books were in English. Then too there were the outstanding moderns whose writings were daily inflating in price: James Joyce, F. Scott Fitzgerald, Ernest Hemingway, J. D. Salinger, and, more recently, the ubiquitous Stephen King. One might speculate in them with more excitement than in the stock market. By the time Y was in his/her thirties, the decision was made. There could be big business in such writings, and Y was all for big business. Why not big book business?

And so, without any extensive education, without any apprenticeship, but with an expert knowledge of price guides to books, Y moved east and set up as a tyro dealer. Funds from the early years in brokerage or computers were applied to an office rental on New York's 57th Street, and its bookshelves were lined with splendid copies of the moderns in first editions, cased neatly in their fine, crisp original jackets. Reference bibliographies informed Y clearly on which page and line of a modern first the letter *h* should take a fall from its brother letters to ensure the presence of a first issue, and Y was serious, diligent, and completely honest about checking on such "points." He/she was prepared and eager for big deals with colleagues or special customers, all of whom appreciated Y's knowledge of stock and erudition about "states." On Y's "Occasional Lists" prices were guaranteed to range from high to so high that they were divulged only "on request." It was not long before this ambitious dealer became eligible to join the Antiquarian Booksellers Association of America, where he/she would play a significant role in educating the public about the value of modern books. As exhibitor at the association's book fairs, Y was sure to follow the wagons to the pot of gold. A goodly portion of the stock he/she sold came from purchases at auctions—including auctions on the Internet.

X and Y differed in many ways, and now even their vocabularies were different. Our old friend X thought a web was woven by a spider, and he could not translate the simple expression *dot com.* To X, *on line* meant straightforward, ready, on the mark. Y was abreast if not in advance of his age and for several years had been an aficionado of the computer world. An insider on the Internet, he spoke its idiom and personified its traits.

We ourselves did not even pretend a familiarity with the complexities of the Internet. Principally, we were aware that it might pose a threat to our accustomed world, and we tried to push it into the background. Someday we would join that world, but not just yet. Meanwhile, in the winter of the year 2000, we were induced to place a bid in an Internet auction. Our observations and reactions reflect our point of view.

The book in question was *The Woman's Bible,* written in 1895 by the eighty-year-old suffrage leader

Elizabeth Cady Stanton, who three years later added a second volume. In her work she analyzed and reinterpreted the derogatory remarks made about women in the Bible. Her comments aroused considerable protest even from some suffragists themselves, who disavowed connection with the Stanton opus. We believed *The Woman's Bible,* as a feminist manifesto, would fit into our holdings, and we decided to make what we considered an appropriate bid on it. Having ascertained that its owner had placed a reserve on it of way under $100, we entered our bid of $960 with some hope of success. The on-line auction, www.ebay.com, ended on March 1. The successful bidder, we were informed, had paid over $12,000 for the prize. Needless to say, our bidding had been performed not by us—we were not yet electronically connected, so to speak—but by a friend. After we learned the results of the auction, we began to think more deeply about what it signified to us.

There had been no details available regarding the authenticity of the work being auctioned. Nothing to assure us that the volumes had been collated—checked for completeness—no bibliographical references vouchsafed—nothing to indicate that a supervisor, an editor, an authority, had taken a hand in the offering. In addition to this lack of a controlling force, there was the astronomical price, which flabbergasted us. To us, who had sold books printed in 1495 for far less than $12,000, it seemed staggering, not on line but out of line.

The Woman's Bible, sold by a mysterious electronic process on ebay, gave these two old-timers much food for thought. There was no doubt that we were living in the midst of a technological revolution. We were more familiar with the one that had occurred five hundred years before. Gutenberg's adaptation of printing by movable type had transformed manuscript into printed book. It had created an artifact that lured the reader, informed the scholar, and pleased the collector. And in accomplishing all that, it had not obliterated the manuscript upon which the book was based. That revolution had spread education, widened horizons, democratized readerships.

What of this current revolution? Would an on-line America discard the printed book? Would the book as we knew and loved it, turning its leaves, devouring its words, holding its binding in our hands, would the book become obsolete, the Age of the Book become the Age of the Dinosaur? How could we reanimate the past on an information superhighway? Could the physical relationship between human being and electronic screen compare with the relationship between human being and bound book? Could we curl up at night with a laptop information retriever and relive a history, read and reread a story?

We two feel that together we personify the Age of the Book, and if our Age has come to an end, so have we. And so we *must* believe that, just as the printed book did not obliterate the manuscript, the Internet will not annihilate the printed book. The Bible makes mistakes, as Elizabeth Cady Stanton pointed out, but it has also been a true prophet. Ecclesiastes tell us: "Of making many books there is no end." And even as we two join the multitudes who click for information on a screen, we shall continue to turn to the books we love and to believe that the Age of the Book is everlasting.

De Canibus Britannicis, liber unus [*A book on English Dogs*], John Caius, Latin, 1729

The earliest treatise on English dogs (first published in 1570). Our eighteenth-century edition testifies to the unceasing popularity of the subject. Bound in three-quarter morocco.

Acquired by a private collector in 1949

Chapter Seven
OUR CANINE SUCCESSION

For nearly all the changes in our lives, the different stages of struggle and triumph, there were dogs in the background or the foreground. Their presence was initiated by Leona, but Madeleine easily became an eager partner in this as in all else. The canine succession began with Skeezie.

If it is possible for an animal to represent the turmoil in a human being's life, then Skeezie was such an animal. In 1925, he came with memories of a rope around his neck and with memories of abandonment. Adolph, Jr., spending a summer in Bear Mountain as counselor at a boys' camp, had found him—a battered cross between collie and shepherd—rescued him, and brought him home to the Bronx house. It was just around the time that Babette had been installed there as the Rostenbergs' housekeeper. She too had memories, memories of the Germany she had left and the losses she had suffered in World War I and its aftermath. Both Skeezie and Babette were lonely, displaced, frightened. Babette showed her fear by talking as little as possible; Skeezie showed his by hiding whenever he could. Neither wished to communicate, but both were aware that in their fear of interacting with the family, they were connecting with each other. Babette and Skeezie comforted each other, loved each other, until they felt at last at home. Leona was drawn into this relationship at a time when she had begun to search for self, for identity, for purpose. The trio seemed to have a magical healing power for one another. Skeezie hid no longer. Indeed, he was soon capable of patrolling outdoors on his own, and he became a happy prowler indeed, winning renown as the great Bronx seducer, sire of innumerable offspring. It should be added that Skeezie also developed a reputation as somewhat of an inebriate, for Babette invariably shared her nightly beer with her companion. Skeezie came to be a kind of paterfamilias, loved by all, including Jean Christophe, the resident cat, who greeted him every morning with three paw pats on his whiskered cheeks. Skeezie lived till he was eighteen. In the course of his long and eventful career he became not only a venerable presence in the big house but a source of comfort to those who needed comfort.

Skeezie was still very much the canine head of house when Leona's own true dog entered the picture. Chimpie arrived in June 1934, when Leona was breaking her relations with Karl, when Madeleine was abroad with her mother, when the Ph.D. candidate was trying to interest herself in Professor Thorndike's *History of Magic.* Born to next-door neighbors, the tiny wire-haired terrier with tan face and black back became Leona's at age ten weeks. Unlike Skeezie, he had no unhappy memories, and unlike Skeezie, he was less the family dog than Leona's very own. Tending the little puppy assuaged loneliness and was an antidote to the complexities of human relationships. For Leona, at that particular time, Chimpie was release from pain, entrée to joy. She tended him and walked him; she cuddled him and talked to him; he slept beside her and trotted beside her. He was her playtoy. Most of all, he was her child, a child to fondle, to spoil, and to love. Chimpie quickly responded to Leona's mothering, becoming a naughty barker and a loyal companion. Where she was, he was always sure to be. As Leona's diary put it, "Every trick of his is refreshing & delightful—my little darling I suppose becoz you're completely mine—Imagine how I'd love a child." Almost from the beginning Leona appreciated Chimpie's intellectual interests. Shortly after his arrival, she wrote in her diary: "He throws his small head back & dances, shouting wildly as he tears across from room to room. I believe he will be an etymologist, as he only tears at my dictionary." Actually, Chimpie's literary interests would widen in the future until they embraced printed matter of all kinds.

The Chimpie years were also the years when we two were strengthening our ties of friendship, and in that too he played an important part. For us together he represented our early carefree relationship, not only in the big Bronx house, but in Maine, where we three spent half a dozen hilarious summers. There, he was heir to all the beefsteaks we ruined on our improvised charcoal grill. There, he played model for the fancy clothes we draped over him and patiently sported the summer hat we set on his tousled brown head. As he grew older, he became an ideal companion for all our summer adventures. He sat right next to Leona in the dory when we rowed across the tidal river from our cottage to the ocean beach. And if we lingered too long in the village and were forced to abandon the little boat to an unanticipated low tide, he stalwartly and courageously walked home with us along U.S. Route 1, usually walking backward and tugging the leash in his mouth. Everywhere we went, Chimpie went with us, always close to his Leona. He was our companion in garbage dump or bookstore, waiting patiently while we disposed of trash or browsed for books at the House of the Thousand Chairs.

Extraordinarily loving with Leona, and serenely tolerant of all human beings, with other dogs Chimpie became a ferocious beast. Madeleine was regularly assigned the task of warning other dog walkers, "Our dog is a fighter, so hold on to your leash." The command was not always heeded. One summer in Maine while we three were ambling along the scenic Marginal Way, overlooking the ocean in Ogunquit, a man approached with three dogs in tow. No sooner had Madeleine issued her ukase about Chimpie than she disappeared into a quartet of quadrupeds, her faint plea for help identifying her for once in her life as underdog.

Chimpie shared our adventures during our Maine summers and our New York winters. In Maine, he accompanied us when we bought books, and he was witness when Leona indited her announcement of the opening of Leona Rostenberg—Rare Books. In New York, Chimpie was present when Leona sold Arthur Young's *Six Weeks Tour through the Southern Counties of England and Wales* to the New York Public Library and so launched her new business. Chimpie was many things: a petted and spoiled child for Leona; a witness to the cementing of our friendship; a founding member of our firm—three weighty identities for a small wire-haired terrier to assume.

After Chimpie's death, in 1946, his place was taken—not entirely successfully—by the next canine incumbent of the Bronx house. A beautiful little Irish terrier, he was Madeleine's gift to Leona, but intellectually he was no peer of his predecessor, Chimpie. Of course we did not know that when he arrived in 1947. That was the year we issued one of our early major catalogues, *The House of Elzevier,* devoted in its entirety to the publications of the great seventeenth-century Dutch firm. Hence there was no question about naming the pet. We called him after one of the principal partners in the Leyden establishment: Bonaventure Elzevier Stern Rostenberg. It was a long name for a puppy, so we shortened it to Bonnie. But it turned out that we could do nothing to sharpen Bonnie's literary—not to mention his publishing—interests. Such rapport as he did have evinced little understanding and no discrimination.

Indeed, it was not more than a year after his arrival that we offered to the Folger Shakespeare Library a sixteenth-century Medici edict on regulations pertaining to streets and boulevards. Among its stipulations was one prohibiting free access of cats and dogs, which may possibly have aroused the rancor of Bonaventure Elzevier. At all events, after Folger had accepted our offer of the edict, we found it on the floor, torn neatly in half. What to do? We phoned the then librarian, our friend "Molly" Pitcher, and informed her of the sad fact, embroidering it a bit by explaining that it had been torn by a "Renaissance whippet." Molly was, as always, quick on the trigger. "A Renaissance whippet named Bonnie Elzevier," she quipped. "Send it on anyway. We'll have it restored."

The incident whetted Bonnie's taste for early printed matter, and he satisfied it on several Renaissance pamphlets and volumes as the years passed. He really had little in common with the original Bonaventure, except perhaps for his whiskers. These were seldom groomed, and as a result, Bonnie looked more like a ragamuffin than a pedigreed Irish terrier. On one occasion, however, when he was about two, Leona had him beautifully groomed. When he was brought home, no one recognized him. Indeed, Dr. Rostenberg—never an admirer of Leona's pets—looked the magnificent creature over and remarked to his daughter, "Now that's the kind of a dog you *should* have!"

Despite his lack of intellectual appreciation for rare books, Bonnie did live through years of development and crisis for us. Dr. Rostenberg's death, our earliest book hunts abroad, the brisk expansion of our business—all these formed the background of his life. During those seminal years he was always there, to be petted for his charm or chastised for his misdemeanors. He was there until 1958, one of the climactic years for us, the year Madeleine's mother died and Madeleine and Leona began their lives together in the big house. Not long after, the Dachshund Dynasty began.

The dynasty started with Cocoa, and it started as a result of the postal operations of Leona Rostenberg—Rare Books. When Madeleine moved up to the Bronx after her many years in Manhattan, she felt she had moved to a small village. Indeed, she frequently compared it to Cranford, the English village fictionalized by Mrs. Gaskell. Everyone seemed to know everyone else, and Madeleine was soon on a first-name basis with baker and grocer, druggist and stationer. Unlike Manhattan, where mail was deposited at one's door, Bronx village life necessitated, for a business like ours, a daily morning visit to the post office. This became part of the day's routine, and Madeleine enjoyed walking downhill to the Jerome

Avenue branch to pick up letters and packages addressed to Leona Rostenberg—Rare Books. Naturally, she picked it all up every day at the same window, where the same postman presided. We were both on a first-name basis with him.

We got to know Bill Levine quite well and soon learned that he had a sideline. Besides being a postal worker, Bill was a breeder of dachshunds. Having experienced the joys of several terriers, we were not prepared for the attractions of dogs so close to the ground. But one day Bill Levine brought to his post office window a baby dachshund, a female, eight weeks old, with smooth hair the color of crème café. The puppy was irresistible. Two weeks later she was ours, and our Dachshund Dynasty was off to a noisy start. Having named our baby Cocoa, with an *a* at the end, we listened to her cry for four days and four nights, weeping for her Bill, who would pay her a visit from time to time. After those four homesick days, Cocoa suddenly ceased her tears and became ours—our Cocoa—our Dachshund Number 1. Thanks to Cocoa, we would come to believe that, for us, there was no other type of dog. Her short legs, her long look, her huge brown trusting eyes, her nosiness, her affection, endeared this "badger hound" to us and committed us to dachshunds for good.

It is, however, undeniable that Cocoa lacked Chimpie's bookish interests. Cocoa was basically a play girl, and as such she rose to her heights when she was our summer companion in the country. By the 1960s we had begun to vacation in East Hampton, and we would continue to rent a cottage near Gardiner's Bay every summer for decades to come. We had selected East Hampton at the suggestion of our feminist customer and now dear friend, Miriam Holden, who, with her husband, Arthur, owned a large house in Quogue, along with a very well-behaved pug named Mingo. One summer during the early 1960s, the Holdens invited the three of us for Sunday dinner in their imposing home on its private beach. In the course of the day we dined leisurely on stuffed roast turkey and apple pie, stroked the sedate Mingo, discussed Miriam's latest finds and our latest acquisitions, reminisced about the suffrage movement, compared notes on swimming and croquet, and suddenly, in the midst of after-dinner coffee, realized that Cocoa had left not only Mingo but her hopeful place under the table. We rose abruptly—we two and Miriam—and immediately separated to conduct individual scouting tours of the house. Before long we heard from a distance Miriam Holden's polite but slightly incredulous and derogatory cry: "Oh, I see Cocoa *has* been here." For us, the deduction was a simple one. Cocoa had been "here," wherever "here" was, and left her unfortunate traces. When "here" turned out to be Miriam's bedroom, we were, of course, abashed, made our apologies and our amends as best we could, and, with the culprit in tow, departed Quogue for East Hampton.

Less than a week later, Cocoa received by post a small book from Mingo Holden, its title: *Prayers for Small Creatures*. There was no actual prayer on the precise subject of Cocoa's misdemeanor, but there was a great deal in the prayers about obedience and discipline, attention and good conduct. Cocoa got the point and, despite her lack of literary talent, decided to thank the sender in verse. From such humble beginnings the Cocoa—Mingo Correspondence developed, becoming in time rather voluminous, including photographs as well as missives. A brief specimen of Cocoa's poetic efforts suffices to indicate the independent feminist attitude she had inherited from us and expressed throughout this curious archive:

I'VE READ YOUR PRAYERS, SO SWEET AND GOLDEN;
MANY THANKS, DEAR MINGO HOLDEN.

BUT PRACTICE WHAT YOU PREACH, BY JINGO,
AND THAT'S MY ANSWER, MR. MINGO.

It was Cocoa, Dachshund Number 1, who moved with us from the Bronx house to our apartment in Manhattan at the end of the decade. She adapted well to the change, and soon was at home with the sidewalks of New York and the small creatures she encountered there. But Cocoa was nearing the end of her days by then, and when we set off on our book hunt abroad in the early 1970s, we left her in the loving care of Edith Wells, secretary of the Antiquarian Booksellers Center, who stayed in our apartment. Edith had no need to tell us about Cocoa's decline when we returned. We could see it all too clearly. But Cocoa, feeble as she was, had matched her independence with her determination. She had waited for us. She died the day after we returned to her.

Cocoa's successor came to us in the summer shortly after we arrived in East Hampton. She appeared with majesty and dignity, qualities that were to characterize both her life and herself. Her breeder drove her all the way from her birthplace in New Jersey, because Madeleine had broken a bone in her foot and was temporarily disabled. As a matter of fact, the new arrival was carried in on a pillow—a tiny, smooth-haired black dachshund with perfect features—and she was carried into a room containing at least a dozen anticipating guests. They may have come to commiserate with Madeleine, who was lying prone on a couch, but they soon transferred their attention to the new arrival.

Most of this dachshund's life would accord with her lofty beginnings. She had come to us just around the time that we were sharing with the public the secrets of Louisa May Alcott's double literary life. More specifically, we had recently edited an anthology of the suspense thrillers by the author of *Little Women*—narratives in which feminist triumph over male chauvinism was a frequent occurrence, along with murder and mayhem. As a result of the publication of *Behind a Mask,* it was unanimously agreed that "never again will you have the same image of this particular little woman." Also as a result of that publication, we named our new baby dachshund Louisa May.

Singularly enough, she not only responded to her name but seemed to take great pride in it. While we two basked in the reflected glory of the Concord Scheherazade, Louisa May Stern Rostenberg seemed to bask in our unexpected renown. Indeed, most of her life she would spend basking when she was not barking. She seemed to understand that, like herself, her name was well beloved.

The brouhaha that attended our exposure of the Alcott literary secrets brought several admirers into our ken. One in particular became a close friend. Actually, Henry Fried had much in common with us, in addition to our mutual passion for biblio-mysteries. He loved books and collected them, especially volumes and pamphlets that traced the history of the

French Revolution. We happened to be well supplied with these, and he was a frequent browser among our shelves. He lived nearby, and we were happy to have a well-wisher within easy reach; he enjoyed the companionship of older women, and no one could doubt that we certainly filled the bill. Best of all, Henry loved dogs, and thanks to a childhood pet, he had a special rapport with dachshunds. The black-haired beauty named Louisa May evoked his intense admiration and returned it ostentatiously. It was obvious to all that the two were deeply in love with each other.

Louisa's later years were enriched by the relationship. When Henry drove us to a book auction in Connecticut or a book fair in New Jersey, Louisa was there, seated next to the driver on the front seat. When he invited us around the corner to his apartment, Louisa was always there with us, heading directly to the kitchen, where a bowl of specially prepared chopped liver awaited Her Highness. She was so involved in our doings by this time that Henry suggested we make her a junior partner, secretary-general of the firm of Rostenberg & Stern.

Her tenure did not last long. Louisa May died in

the mid-1980s. She had lived with us through a period of literary discovery and revelation, and in our eyes she was an inextricable part of all the attendant excitement we had experienced. For us, those years were the years of two extraordinary Louisa Mays.

If possible, the dachshund who followed Louisa was even more closely connected to the book world we inhabited. By the time Bettina became ours, there were few close friends left who doubled as dog lovers. She was ours and ours alone. And she knew this. She made it a habit always to sit between us, whether we occupied a living room sofa or two library chairs. And unlike any of her predecessors, Bettina even sat between us when we appeared on the jacket of a book.

Bettina did not come to us; we came to her. She was one of a small litter bred in New Jersey, and we drove out to fetch her as soon as she was sufficiently mature, that is, nine or ten weeks old. We were introduced first to her grandmother Viola and other members of her family before we were shown our prize. And prize she was—a small, smooth-haired beauty with the same coloring as Cocoa. Leona insisted that she be named after Madeleine but, to avoid confusion, selected Madeleine's middle name, Bettina.

Bettina was a perfect puppy, doing everything one could possibly expect from a puppy and more that one could not expect. She enacted perpetual motion from the time she awoke till about nine P.M., when she simply sat back in complete collapse and fell asleep. In East Hampton, where we accompanied her when she was about six months old, her activity took the form of running away. She ran not to leave us, but simply to express her complete abandon. She knew exactly where she was, and when she was ready, she ran back to us. But never until she was ready. On one occasion she chose to depart just before we were scheduled to lecture before the Round Table. The lecture was postponed until we received word that Lady Bettina had decided to return. She knew precisely what she was doing. She loved us dearly, but she also, especially in her puppydom, loved her exuberant freedom.

As she grew older, the former love triumphed over the latter, to such an extent that she seemed heartbroken when we left her for a few days. In 1992 we were invited to give the keynote address at the

Colorado Seminar on Rare Books. Although Bettina was well and lovingly cared for during our absence, her greeting to us upon our return resembled a sob far more than a cry of happiness. She was simply overwhelmed to have us back again, and she wept her overflowing joy. Bettina was convinced that, wherever we went, she belonged with us. During our East Hampton summers she was the constant companion, whether we visited beach or village, whether we browsed in Canio's Bookshop in Sag Harbor or dropped into shops in Southampton. With Bettina we were no longer a duo. She made us a trio, and she knew it.

She was especially insistent about this when it came to our professional pursuits. Around this time, perhaps in the wake of renewed interest in the Alcott thrillers, we were invited to participate in a British Broadcasting Corporation program on nineteenth-century feminist literary figures. In deference to Louisa Alcott's most powerful thriller, "Behind a Mask: or, A Woman's Power," the whole series was entitled "Behind a Mask." We two provided the Alcott segment, which was videotaped in our apartment. Once Bettina realized what was going on, however, we two became we three. There was absolutely no denying Bettina her part in the program. She insisted upon appearing in person, lying between us as the cameras rolled. If the British broadcasters objected, we heard no complaints. Indeed, after "Behind a Mask" was aired, we received a highly laudatory note from the program directors, ending with the statement: "Bettina is now the TV rage of London."

A few years passed before Bettina acquired her American reputation. Then, in 1995, spurred by an article about us in the *New York Times,* Betsy Lerner, an editor, made that—for us three—most productive of phone calls: "Doubleday wonders if you would be interested in writing a memoir for us." By 1996 the memoir was written and entitled *Old Books, Rare Friends: Two Literary Sleuths and Their Shared Passion.* After due consideration, the publishers decided to place a picture of the literary sleuths on the book's jacket. Only two sleuths had written the memoir; but, as it happened, the portrait of a third appeared on the jacket. Bettina knew that her day had come.

In early spring of 1997, the photographers arrived at the Rostenberg-Stern domain with full equipment and accompanied by the art director, a cosmetician, and a charming young woman whose main purpose seemed to be to hold our skirts at a decorous angle. We were posed in front of a bookcase of rarities, side by side on a small sofa sometimes called a loveseat. Positions were taken, our skirts were held, our expressions were set, and the cameras started to flash. At that moment another flash suddenly occurred, the flash of Bettina's tail as she spryly sprang up on the loveseat exactly between her two loved ones. If we were the center of attention, our dachshund was the center of the center. There was no coaxing her away. And even the photographers agreed that she heightened the interest of the picture. When, every once in a while, Bettina grew restless and turned around, presenting her rear to the camera, the technicians simply waited for her to resume her original position. They obviously thought it worthwhile to have our third on board.

As it turned out, for many many viewers Bettina made the picture. The jacket depicted us sitting in front of rows of books with a brown, smooth-haired dachshund between us, her dark eyes gazing directly at the camera. On our faces are smiles at once proud and joyous, not only for the publication of *Old Books, Rare Friends,* but for the presence on the jacket of darling Bettina, who had been part of it and part of us.

When Bettina died, we knew the time had come for us to put an end to our canine succession. We knew, but we did not believe and could not tolerate the thought. And so, she was followed by a handsome nine-week-old short-haired black male dachshund. The present incumbent, who will soon enter his terrible twos, was named Laurie, in remembrance of the hero of *Little Women.* Laurie is perhaps the most loving of all our pets. He loves all the world and would assuredly welcome intruder by day or thief by night. He will shortly begin to be videotaped in connection with a projected documentary about his mammas, but as of this moment he has not actively participated in any of our professional activities. He has participated in our love, and it is our hope that he will do so for a long time. As he approaches maturity, however, we approach and overreach old age. He loves the world, but so do we, and we do not want to leave him there without us.

Like all our canine succession, Laurie has complemented our lives, connecting with us, enriching us, extending our dimensions. All our dogs, from Skeezie to Chimpie, from Cocoa to Louisa May and Bettina, have been conveyors of joy. But in our canine succession we can no longer look to the future. There is no doubt now that that glorious succession is ending and that Laurie will be the last of the line.

De Bono Senectutis [*On the Good Aspects of Old Age*], Gabriel Paleoti, Latin, 1598

A study of old age emphasizing its happier aspects: fortitude of soul, knowledge and studies of the old, regimen of life. With a portrait of the aged St. Philip of Neri, bound in boards.

Acquired by a colleague
in 1960

Chapter Eight
AGING TOGETHER

To aging eyes, successions do not always end clearly, suddenly, with finality. Change creeps in so gradually at first that it is not recognized. Endings insinuate themselves imperceptibly, in the search for a word or a pair of eyeglasses, a name or a landscape. Louisa Alcott's mother, riding around the city she had known for most of her life, gazed at the unfamiliar and exclaimed, "It's not my Boston anymore!" Now, as we two age together, we would like to take inventory of the changes in our world before change takes over.

Now we can answer the question Leona asked in her diary on June 13, 1931: "What happens as you grow older—, do the doors stay open—shut—or flung wide? I wonder."

Most of the doors—the outside doors—shut slowly but irrevocably. The doors shut when hills rise where they had not existed before—when streets that were once level begin to develop sharp inclines. We find we can no longer run up the steps at 82nd Street and Fifth Avenue, enter the Metropolitan Museum of Art, and wander from gallery to gallery. But we can remember a Goya exhibit there that was followed by a display of grand Monets back in 1938, not only because Leona recorded it in her diary, but because we ended up unfatigued and longing for more. The concerts we do not attend today are replaced by auditory memories. Even as we decide against subscribing to a chamber music series—taxis are too hard to find, buses too slow to arrive, and walk we cannot—we recall the "thrilling concerts" of the past, "brilliantly performed by first-rate musicians." And strains of Brahms' Second Piano Concerto played by José Iturbi reverberate in our inward ears, followed by young Yehudi Menuhin playing Brahms' Violin Concerto with the New York Philharmonic.

Most of the second balconies we rushed to half a century ago are located now not on, but off Broadway, and if the theaters have curtains, they seldom rise on such actors as those who enchanted us:

Katharine Cornell, Judith Anderson, Bea Lillie, the Barrymores, that delicious duo Alfred Lunt and Lynn Fontanne. If we have changed, so have our performers and so has the offered fare. We seldom find, even in revival, plays like Thornton Wilder's *Our Town, The Dark at the Top of the Stairs, The Barretts of Wimpole Street, Watch on the Rhine, You Can't Take It with You.* We no longer race up the steps of a theater; we cannot. It is the magic of a remembered stage that transports us now.

That magic transports us also to the balcony of the cinema, where we smoke and chew gum, smoke and munch chocolate, smoke and stare at the screen, seeing perhaps John Gilbert and Greta Garbo. Afterward we rush to Schrafft's or a cafeteria, where we discuss the picture over coffee and a cigarette, inevitably ending our movie critiques with plans, real or imaginary, to go abroad.

If finding a seat in a darkened theater presents an insurmountable challenge for us today, how much more difficult have become the problems of travel. Travel, once endowed with so many elegancies, has become a completely self-service affair, with which we cannot cope. Extricating luggage from a holding area, carrying it to the street, finding transport—even when the destination is domestic and not European—has become too much for us. But we cannot help recalling with delight the travels of our past.

We can no longer take the train to Boston, as we did in Christmas week of 1938, change there for Cambridge, settle in at the Brattle Inn, and walk down Tory Row. But we can remember passing the home of Dunster Pratt, whose spreading chestnut tree inspired Mr. Longfellow in the Craigie Mansion. And we still have the letter penned on December 23 by the catering manager of Boston's Hotel Touraine to Dear Miss Stern, who had written to reserve a table in honor of Leona's birthday on the twenty-eighth. The means of communication, the style of writing, the contents of the note encapsulate a *temps passé*, a time that cannot be replicated:

> *We are in receipt of your letter of December 21st, [he wrote], from which we note that you contemplate entertaining a friend of yours on Wednesday evening, December 28th, in*

our Grill. We will be glad to reserve a table for you if you will be kind enough to let us know the time of your arrival.

A steak dinner may be had for $2.00 per person or Roast Ribs of Beef dinner at $1.35, or Lamb Chops dinner for $1.35 . . . this to include an appetizer, dessert and coffee.

If you wish to send flowers for your table, you may address them, with your name, to the writer and I will be glad to see that they are placed on the table.

Hoping that we shall be favored with your patronage and with the Season's Greetings, we remain . . .

Mario V. Bertolini, Catering Manager, does indeed remain—but only in our files and in our memory.

Foreign travel today has become literally foreign to our way of life. We began our European expeditions on shipboard, and took a week or ten days to arrive at our destination. Aboard the S.S. *California,* we sat at the top of the vessel, almost midway between sea and sky, and we reveled in both at the same time. When we were courageous enough to attempt the crossing by plane, the flight took thirteen hours, at least six of them devoted to sound sleep and several of them to the consumption of delicious cooked meals. Later, we endured as long as we could the discomfort that accompanied speed, but when the former far surpassed the latter, and our own adaptability diminished, we stopped physical locomotion and substituted the mental kind. We who have walked Paris's Left Bank so often, London's Strand, the Boboli Gardens in Florence, the Foro Romano, Vienna's Prater, even the Kanda in Tokyo—walk today the less strenuous streets of memory.

Those streets do not change in remembrance, but the streets where we live do. Hills appear where we did not notice them before; signs change; proprietors disappear; and it's not our city anymore. Today the street is filled with rushing walkers with their ubiquitous props—cellular phones—permanently attached to mouths and ears. They wear the air of sloppy discontent in their attire, and they all seem to favor accidental creases rather than permanent pleats, holes cut into garments, tears, and shoddiness. The ultra-casual effect, we understand, has been carefully planned and expensively acquired at fashion establishments entitled the Gap or Banana Republic.

Where have our stores gone? Where is Russeks, where we once bought furs—now all but outlawed; where are Jay Thorpe and Bonwit Teller, Best's and the most exclusive De Pinna? Where, for that matter, are Orbach's and S. Klein on Union Square? They have vanished, along with the styles we sported.

In that connection, where are the dime stores of old—the Woolworths and Lamstons and Kresges—where we could once buy notions and wool, pins and needles, pads and pencils with erasers that erased? They live in limbo and in memory, along with the little independent stores that we patronized for a roll of thread or a paper of hooks and eyes, for a Hershey bar or a fudge sundae at the counter. Where, oh where, is the twirling barber pole that used to adorn the street?

When we two, checking our rare books at the New York Public Library, decided to break for lunch, we walked a block to the 42nd Street Schrafft's and ordered an egg salad sandwich on toasted cheese bread with a coffee milkshake. After we spent an hour or two at a newsreel theater (now a ghost), we dropped into Huyler's or Mirror's for a frosted, and before an evening at Radio City Music Hall, we had dinner at Longchamps—creamed chicken—or the Brass Rail—roast beef.

Where are the snows of yesteryear? Where are the repair shops where even a fountain pen could once undergo resuscitation? They have been replaced by incinerators. With built-in obsolescence an essential, repair has evolved into discard and replace. We miss them all, the shops that punctuated our landscape. Especially we miss the department stores where escalators transported us from oriental rugs to silver, from cutlery to hardware, from delicacies to home furnishings, from tailored suits to evening dresses. The vast emporium of B. Altman provided most of our needs, especially the styles we grew to love: the jacketed dresses, the array of blouses, the straight skirts that we wore until we wore them out. When we try to replace our styles today, we are greeted with questioning raised eyebrows, and we feel almost as defunct as B. Altman & Company.

We know precisely how Mrs. Alcott felt in Boston. Both scene and time have changed as we walk on stage for Act Three. It is not our time anymore, and for that matter it is not our *Times* anymore either—not our *New York Times*. We read the paper together at breakfast, and where we once found in the first paragraph of a story the answers to "Who, What, When, Where, and Why," we now read a narrative, possibly fictional, about some character who may or may not lead us eventually to the consumption of some facts. The exploits of the Yankees take precedence over an Armenian siege in which the prime minister is slain. A lengthy feature story is devoted to an auction at which the dress Marilyn Monroe wore when she sang "Happy Birthday" to President Kennedy was sold for $1.15 million plus commission. No, it is not our *Times* anymore—not the *Times* that really did once give us "All the News That's Fit to Print."

For the most radical of all the changes in our world—the great revolution in electronics—we are especially unprepared. We, who sat comfortably so long before our typewriters, are now overwhelmed with the fear that they too will vanish forever. The thought that the Internet may supersede the book is too devastating for us to dwell upon, other than to reiterate our promise to help guide the book in all its glory into an electronic world. We still buy and sell rare books; we still savor the joys of detection. We still issue catalogues, and we still participate in book fairs. Eagerly we wait for the phone to ring with an order for a book we have offered. And we still write books together. The thought of retirement is repugnant to us both. Despite the changes surrounding us, we love what we do and hope to continue doing it.

At the same time, it is obvious that our reaction to the transformations in our world is occasioned not only by exterior events but by interior ones. In us, too, change has been at work. We frequently forget, not just where we left our keys or our wallets, but a word, a name, even an idea. We are less amenable than formerly; now we resent it when an unknown telephone caller opens with, "Is this Madeleine or Leona—oh, Leona, we hope you are having a nice day," and continues with unwelcome solicitations. And when *we* try to telephone to a government department or a bank, a post office or a corporation, and are regaled with a menu of choices from 1 to 12, with music in between, we become apoplectic. As a result, it has become essential for us to remember to take our blood pressure pills, whose intimidating names we long since consigned to oblivion.

Actually, we both take the same blood pressure pills, although each of us also has several other prescribed medications, which would add variety to our conversation if we discussed them and their aftereffects. We are more inclined to discuss our physicians and their vagaries, their care or carelessness, and their offices, overwhelmed with the paperwork engendered by bureaucracy. For the most part, we are so busy trying to stay productively alive that we leave these medical soliloquies to friends and acquaintances.

But—alas!—they too are disappearing, one by one. We re-do our address books and strike out names we shall never call again. We re-do our lives to accommodate for absences. Way back in 1943, Leona wrote in her diary: "I realize how my parents are aging—each differently—and the reality of it at times paralyzes me—the very fear & heartache of the thought of life without either of them." The loss of family, of friends, and even of our dogs can only proliferate as we age, leaving so many behind. After our parents, our friends began to follow, one by one, preceding us to oblivion. Most of our colleagues have gathered there—those who not only browsed bookshelves and compared bibliographic notes with us, but dined and wined with us. Claimed by retirement or death, they have left the scene, along with librarians who were our friends and have now been replaced by strangers of another generation.

And so, memory pursues its destined role. As we forget why we came into a room or where we placed a reference book, we remember vividly the rooms, the books, the people of the past. Leona presaged this in an early diary note that recorded our celebration of her birthday in Boston's Hotel Touraine: "A very happy day which, even when the lights are low and the candles flicker . . . will remain bright and indelible." In memory they are still "bright and indelible," the friends and family who have walked off stage.

Productive survival is the fruit of other vital seeds also. As our senses diminish—Leona's sight,

Madeleine's hearing—we see and hear for each other. Over breakfast, Madeleine reads the headlines and the news summary to Leona, dipping into the editorials as Leona drops terse comments into the recital. Later in the day Madeleine reads the mail aloud, interrupted by Leona's exclamations: "Don't bother opening that." "What a waste!" "Throw it out!" until suddenly Madeleine tears open and reads a long epistle from a fan. Then beatific smiles appear on both faces as the delicious compliments resound. The reading aloud continues, especially when the arrival of a favorite bookseller's catalogue stops all other activity, and Madeleine scans the offered items until she lights on one she knows Leona will agree to acquire. "Here's a first edition of Descartes on the passions of the soul—great condition—price not too astronomical—only nine hundred pounds. How about it? Should we order it?"

Throughout the day, when the phone rings, Leona takes over to clarify the gist of a caller's conversation or, more frequently, to convey to Madeleine the string of choices emanating from some electronic automaton. In the afternoons, when an interviewer or a novice bookseller or a prospective customer pays a visit, Leona will repeat for Madeleine voices that have escaped her ears. And in the evening, if there are guests all determined to speak at once, Leona will retail to Madeleine the substance of the talk so that she can resume her part in the conversation.

After such episodes we cannot help recalling the many extraordinary sounds and scenes we have experienced together in the past, when we were both unafflicted by the intrusions of age. Especially we remember the grand combination of sound and spectacle that thrilled ear and eye and reverberates even now—the lavish performance that the French call *Son et Lumière*—Sound and Light. Today, as we see and hear for each other, we are creating our own latter-day *Son et Lumière*. We are also finding security in each other's capabilities. Security has become a bulwark for our weaknesses, and we seek it everywhere, from the roof over our heads to the balance in our bank accounts and the services we have come to need—for carrying groceries or cooking meals, for opening a child-resistant package or taking books to the post office or driving a car in the dark. If memory of the past enriches us, security in the present strengthens us, and together they prepare us for the future.

We who have survived must now seek younger companions. In this we two have been most fortunate. Into our lives have ventured the dramatist who is cogitating a play based on one of our books, the librettist who sees us as characters in a musical, the documentarian who would transport our story to the TV screen. All have been solicitous, warm, and loving—but they did not share our beginnings. We cannot smile knowingly with them as we recall the rich past.

Next to memory and security, perhaps even ahead of them, it is work that dilutes the effects of aging. In this we two have been blessed. Together we have transferred our lives, our fixations, our eccentricities, our intensities, to the written page, and in the transference we have been able to endure the intrusions of aging. Leona's earliest diaries reflect the tales she imagined and the titles of her stories: "The Rag," "Chance," "Coming Home." Madeleine began writing almost as soon as she could dip pen into ink. Lifelong habits have continued, bringing us both survival.

If that survival is often irradiated with joy, it is thanks to the word *both* in its context. By living together we have made aging a feasible, even an acceptable process. By writing together we have created a strong fabric out of life's innumerable disparate threads.

Bookends is not only the title of this book. It is our very nature. Bookends support books and come in pairs. And that is the life we have led. If the word encapsulates our past, it looks also to the future, and to the books—lived together, written together—that will follow.

ACKNOWLEDGMENTS

We are indebted, first, to the cast of characters who made our history and people this book.

Second, although *Bookends* really wrote itself, particular individuals helped shape it, and we are grateful to them: our dedicatee, Helen Keppler Miller, the friend who remembers the past and shares the present; Katharine Houghton, actress and dramatist, who is tracing our lives through our letters and journals; Abbey Lustgarten, our documentarian, for her photographs of our family oil paintings; Betsy Lerner, our literary agent, whose understanding and acumen placed this book just where it belonged; Frances Apt, our incomparable copyeditor, who knows when and how to improve; and especially our editor at The Free Press, Chad Conway, whose insight is intuitive and whose critical skills are creative.

239

INDEX

Index

74, 83, 85, 94, 115, 116,
140, 142, 165
Extension, 69
Graduate School of Political
Science, 73
Concord, Massachusetts, 143,
213
Cornell, Katharine, 225
Corrigan, Lillian, 53
Cowan, Alvin, 61, 96
Cromack, Miss, 53

Dalton, Florence, 53
*Dark at the Top of the Stairs,
The*, 225
Depression, national, 57, 63, 73,
91
Dictionary of Literary Biography,
177
Dolet, Etienne, 190
Doubleday & Company, 218
Dreyfus, Bertha Hirsch, 11, 12.
See also Hirsch, Bertha
Dreyfus, David, 7–8
Dreyfus, Josephine, 18
Dreyfus, Leah Johanna Frank, 7
Dreyfus, Leon, 8–9, 10, 11, 12,
15, 17, 18, 19, 20, 29, 34
Dreyfus, Louisa, 12, 17–19,
20–22, 29–33, 149. *See also*
Rostenberg, Louisa Dreyfus
birth, 12
marriage, 33
portrait of, 21
volunteer work, 21–22, 29
Dreyfus, Theodore, 8
Dreyfus family, 7, 19
Dutton, E. P. and Company, 144

East Hampton, New York,
209, 210, 212, 216,
217
Electronic Age, 2–3, 193–196,
231–232
Elzevier Press, 205
Emanu-El, Temple, 12, 15, 22,
26, 49, 58
Sabbath School, 58–60, 70,
71–72, 78
Sunday School, 48–50, 51, 55,
57, 58
Enelow, H. G., 49, 50
Ephemera, 172–173
Erasmus, Desiderius, 119
Evander Childs High School, 67,
69, 188

Fairchild, Hoxie, 43, 56
Falconia Proba, Valeria, 168
Centones, 168
Feminism, 90, 135, 159–178,
181–196
Fitzgerald, F. Scott, 191
Flanter, Karl, 110–116, 124, 125,
201
Florence, Italy, 70, 164,
228
Folger Shakespeare Library, 90,
205
Fontanne, Lynn, 225
French Revolution, 163, 214
Freud, Sigmund, 79
Fried, Henry, 213–214
Froelich's school, 23
Fuller, Margaret, 165, 169
*Woman in the Nineteenth
Century*, 169

241

Index

Index